Cat's Meat Square

Housing and Public Health
in South St Pancras 1810-1910

Stephen W Job

© Camden History Society
and the author 2012

ISBN 978 0 904491 85 2

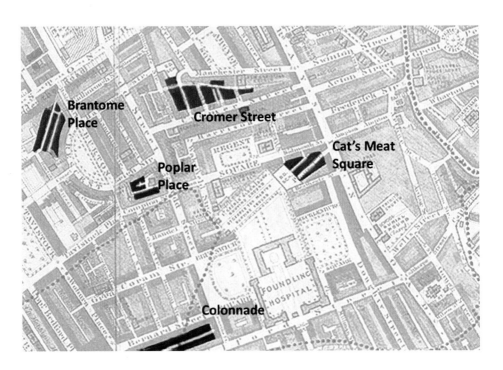

"Cat's Meat Square" and other black spots in Ward 8 of St Pancras in the mid-1880s.
From the 1889 edition of Charles Booth's poverty maps of London.
Black areas correspond to Booth's dark blue and black.

Cat's Meat Square

Housing and Public Health in South St Pancras 1810-1910

Stephen W Job

Edited by F Peter Woodford

Designed by Ivor Kamlish

Published by Camden History Society   2012

The area which earned the sobriquet Cat's Meat Square is the tiny triangle south of Sidmouth Street which includes Wellington Square, Derry Street and Prospect Terrace (OS 1871)

Contents

Illustrations

Sources

Nos.1, 3: British History Online

Nos.4, 6-8, 11, 13, 21-27: Camden Local Studies and Archives Centre

Nos.10, 16, 18, 30: London Metropolitan Archives

No.12: Museum of London

No.14: National Portrait Gallery

No.17: Based on Charles Booth's Poverty Map of London, 1889

Nos.28, 29: English Heritage

1 Introduction

If one looks at the rebuilt Westminster Kingsway College from the quiet haven of St George's Gardens, it may be tempting to think that the college site has always been associated with education. Not so: the view from the gardens in the 19th century would have been very different. Approximately half of the site, a triangle of less than an acre, was once home to 900 people in some of the worst housing conditions in south St Pancras.

This small knot of streets lay west of Gray's Inn Road and south of Sidmouth Street, and included Prospect Terrace, Wellington Square and James Street (Derry Street from 1865). Built in the 1810s on part of the Harrison Estate, by the 1870s these streets had achieved such notoriety as an overcrowded, insanitary rookery that they were known locally as 'Cat's Meat Square'. They were demolished in 1906 and replaced by Prospect Terrace Flats, one of three housing developments undertaken by St Pancras Borough Council in the Edwardian period. Part of Wellington Square had already been replaced by a Board School in the 1880s. All would in turn fall victim to the Blitz in WWII, and after the war the site became wholly used for education.

The story of Cat's Meat Square reflects the rise and decline of similar neighbourhoods throughout London between 1800 and the early 1900s, and the progress of housing and sanitary reform in south St Pancras as a whole. But this tiny development of low-grade housing was unusual in two ways: it included a purpose-built back-to-back terrace – a rarity in London – and a diminutive square. The question arises: did the Harrison Estate envisage this development from the outset as working-class housing, or did it have grander aspirations?

Most histories of London housing focus on the slums of east London and Southwark. In the borough of St Pancras, Agar Town and Somers Town are familiar to local historians; less so the small pockets of poor housing that developed south of the Euston Road, particularly in Ward 8 of the borough. In a swathe of London north of the old centre running from St Luke's and Clerkenwell through south St Pancras and Holborn, pockets of extreme poverty existed surrounded by relative comfort. Sir Charles Dilke, chairman of the Royal Commission on Housing of the Working Classes (1885), considered that some of the worst social conditions in the country could be found in these pockets, and Prospect Terrace, Derry Street and

Wellington Square all featured in evidence to the Royal Commission. A few years later, Charles Booth was to mark these areas dark blue and black on his poverty maps of London (see p 2).

The pattern of property ownership here is complex. The process of tracking the builders and leaseholders of Cat's Meat Square and the neighbouring slum areas uncovers a host of 'house farmers', as they came to be known, as well as their sometimes suspicious links to the St Pancras Vestry (the predecessor of the Borough Council). The reports of successive highly competent local Medical Officers of Health over the decades provide insight into conditions in the houses, the officers' valiant efforts towards sanitary reform and their tussles with house farmers and the vestry. Later, Cat's Meat Square was the subject of battles between the Vestry and the London County Council over what to do about the area and, more importantly, whose responsibility it was.

I have tried in this biography of the area to paint a picture of the evolution of workers' housing and social policy in south St Pancras from the days of the Regency through to Edwardian times. Historical records, newspaper reports and photographs afford a glimpse of life at different times in Cat's Meat Square. The area supported a large Irish population, unfairly singled out at times as the cause of its decline. What was, actually, the real social makeup of this and other insanitary areas in Ward 8? The last days of Cat's Meat Square saw off the worst slums in that part of the borough, but where did the inhabitants go after the evictions of 1906?

2 Burials and brickfields: the development of Prospect Terrace

(Notes for this chapter on p 15)

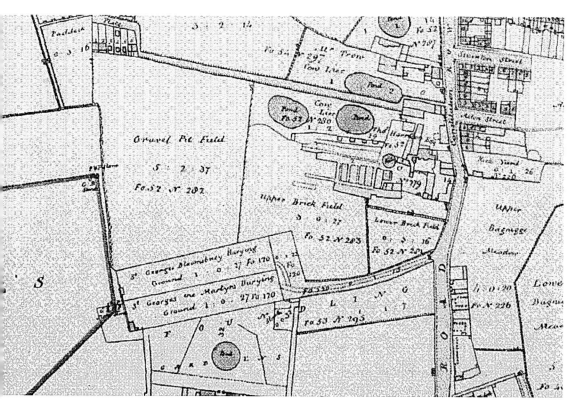

[1] Part of John Thompson's map of St Pancras of 1803 showing the Harrison Estate and its brickworks. The burial grounds of St George's Bloomsbury and St George the Martyr (now St George's Gardens) lay to the south, and beyond them the Foundling Estate. The access way to the graveyards from Gray's Inn Lane was known as Prospect Place and originally had a fine view southwards.

The Prospect Terrace area emerged as part of the Regent Square development on the Harrison Estate. The Harrison property lay north and east of the Foundling Estate and the burial grounds of St George's Bloomsbury and St George the Martyr. The eastern boundary of the estate was formed by Gray's Inn Lane (now Road), with the Lucas Estate to the north and the Skinners' Estate to the northwest [1]. The Harrison family, originally farmers, had developed the modest 13-acre estate as a brickfield throughout the 18th century, supplying the constant demand for bricks as nearby estates were transformed into housing. The giant dust heap at King's Cross lying to the north supplied the brickworks with cinders.

Thomas Harrison [2] inherited the estate in 1783 and by the start of the new century had decided to join the development boom. He drew up plans to create what was to become Regent Square; Sidmouth Street was to run along its south side to Gray's Inn Lane and Harrison Street to the north of the Square. Harrison was comparatively late in turning to building development – the brickworks had provided a good income – but by this time constructing houses was becoming more lucrative. However, the layout of the grid forming Regent Square and surrounding streets on Harrison's plan created an awkward wedged-shaped piece of land south of Sidmouth Street and north of the access way to the burial grounds, Prospect Place. The access way dated from 1713 and was not in the ownership of either the Foundling or the Harrison estates but belonged to the two churches.

This small wedge of land, about two thirds of an acre, was to become the Prospect Terrace area. The configuration of the land was less than optimal for the sort of medium-quality housing Harrison projected for Regent Square and its neighbouring streets. Stabling and basic dwellings for servants were usually in mews behind principal streets or in minor streets nearby, but the piece of land south of Sidmouth Street did not fit this pattern. Solving the problem of what to build there led Harrison to adopt an unusual building form for London, probably devised by his surveyor, Thomas Spencer.

Harrison showed his plan to Samuel Pepys Cockerell, surveyor to the Foundling Estate, who was evidently unimpressed: in 1802 he advised[1] his Estate to construct a new road to the north of the Foundling Hospital, to connect Brunswick Square and (the projected) Mecklenburgh Square and to protect these 'respectable quarters' from exposure to 'the inferior and irregular buildings which will probably be built northward of them'. In 1807 he again referred to Harrison's buildings as 'of so mean and inferior a quality' that they would discredit the Foundling Estate.[2] Harrison was also accused of trying to connect up with the Foundling streets without payment. Cockerell's successor, Joseph Kay, was also in favour of a new street with a terrace of housing, thereby 'shutting out the present dead wall to the burying ground and the back fronts of the buildings rising on Mr Harrison's ground'.[3] Only Heathcote Street was eventually constructed, complete with gates, and its back gardens ran up to the burial grounds roadway (see [3]).

10

[3] A view of the Foundling Hospital c.1808, almost certainly drawn from the junction of Prospect Place and Gray's Inn Lane. This field was to become Heathcote Street, Mecklenburgh Street and part of Mecklenburgh Square, with Prospect Terrace to the right and behind the viewpoint.

The Foundling Hospital

On Harrison's plan, Wellington Place was to provide vehicular access off the unfinished Sidmouth Street leading to a small square of 18 houses with a grassed area in the middle. A short cul-de-sac street of a further 18 houses, to be called James Street (on later maps shown as Derry Street), was to lead off to the east, and backed onto these and the south side of the square was to be a further terrace of 15 houses, connected only by footways to the square. A public house, the Prince Regent, was proposed for the corner of Sidmouth Street and Wellington Place, which would also contain two shops.

Access for carts to the Prospect Terrace development was not possible directly from Gray's Inn Lane because the churches owned the roadway and would allow only hearses and mourners to use it. Harrison may have attempted to acquire the access way or to come to an accommodation with the churches, but he clearly failed to do so and had to make the best of the irregular plot. The original sketches in the Middlesex Deeds Register (MDR) confirm the intention to build Prospect Terrace back-to-back with James Street, with only pedestrian access from Gray's Inn Road and two narrow alleys from Wellington Square and the middle of James Street. Had Harrison managed to secure the roadway, it might have been narrowed from its generous 34ft width, and Prospect Terrace may never have been built back-to-back. There was apparently no agreed right of way over the roadway, which remained unpaved and the source of much dispute over responsibility for its upkeep for a century.

Undaunted, Harrison pressed on. He petitioned parliament in February 1810 and a Paving Act was passed two months later[4]; a few houses on Gray's Inn Lane (one of which was occupied by Harrison until 1809) had already been built and others started. Harrison agreed a series of leases in 1810 and 1811 for plots on the greater part of Sidmouth Street, Harrison Street and Prospect Terrace, primarily with James Payne, one of the builders of Marchmont Street.[5] In 1809 Payne had signed building leases with the Skinners' Company for parts of Leigh Street and Tonbridge Place, and he was clearly intended to be the lead builder of the Harrison Estate. His brother George was also a local developer[6]; he was particularly active on the Foundling Estate and was responsible for parts of Mecklenburgh Square. They may have been related to another lessee of one small plot in Prospect Terrace, William Payne.[7] He is described as a yeoman of Euston Hall, Suffolk, seat of the Duke of Grafton, a local landowner. One plot of ten houses on the south side of the intended square was leased to an Edward Carr of Glamorgan.[8]

The houses were constructed from 1810, possibly late 1809, and the first 13 formed the northern half of Wellington Square; they appear in the rate books from January 1812.[9] The northern side of James Street followed, with the first Prospect Terrace/ James Street houses appearing in the rate books in 1817, although Joseph Kay clearly refers to the 'back fronts' (which must mean the back-to-backs) rising in 1811.

Payne subcontracted at least some of the building work, and a surveyor's affidavit of March 1810 confirmed that '13 houses built by John Knight' for James Payne south of Sidmouth Street met the requirements of the Building Act.[10] It is likely that this is the same John Knight, of Kenton Street, thought to be responsible for part of Euston Square. There would undoubtedly have been others, but more established builders such as James Burton do not seem to have ventured onto the Harrison Estate, perhaps with good reason. The Payne brothers both became founding members of the Harrison Estate Paving Commission (established by the 1810 Act), as did John Knight.[11] Within months, however, there were signs that James Payne was suffering ill-health, and his accounts were said to be not 'in a completed state'. In May 1811 the paving contractor for Sidmouth Street told the Commissioners that he could not continue because of Payne 'not having completed the vaults' to his houses.[11] James Payne was responsible for paving much of the development himself, but by February 1813 the new pavement in front of Prospect Terrace had been removed by creditors and the works were said to be in a 'ruinous and dangerous state'.[11] This may explain why the Terrace does not appear in the rate books until 1817.

James Payne had moved into Wellington Square from Marchmont Street with his wife Jane and family shortly after the first houses were finished, almost certainly more because business was turning sour than out of preference – Marchmont Street would have been a better address. In March 1813 he was paid £7 15s 'in full' by the Commissioners for paving Wellington Square but by April 1813 he was listed as bankrupt[12], possibly because of his illness, incompetence and being unable to lease on enough properties. Another small builder, Benjamin Bennett of 10 Wellington Square, had been declared bankrupt the previous November.[13]

The price of building materials doubled during the Napoleonic wars, putting huge pressure on builders, especially the smaller variety of which Payne was almost certainly one. Small developers depended on rapid turnover, either of completed houses or as carcases for other small builders to finish, and the rate books consistently show many empty houses in Payne's development throughout the 1810s. An advertisement in *The Times* in October 1811 was already offering unfinished houses in Wellington Square and James Street[14] as part of 19 lots of 'valuable and singularly improvable leasehold property, most eligibly situated in a respectable neighbourhood' and in March 1813, just before Payne's bankruptcy, a number of carcases in Wellington Square, Prospect Terrace and Harrison Street were advertised.[15]

Further misfortune struck when James Payne died in October 1815 aged 39.[16] A deathbed will dated 24 October[17] left his estate to his wife, and it does appear that Jane Payne managed to hang on to a substantial number of the leaseholds, which suggests that the bankruptcy had been at least partly discharged. She was living at No.7 Wellington Square in the 1820s[18] and was to stay in the area for the rest of her life: she is described in the 1851 census as a "Proprietor of houses" and residing at No.1 Harrison Street, one of the original Payne leaseholds. To complicate matters, Harrison agreed an assignment of ground rents to Thomas Rhodes in 1819 for some of the development, including parts of Sidmouth Street and six houses in James Street but not Prospect Terrace, probably to raise funds.[19] The Harrison and Rhodes families had a long history of cousin marriages and it is unlikely that this agreement altered the family ownership of the estate at this time. Horwood's map of London of the same year ([4], p 14) shows the slow progress of the development.

It was not until 1824 that all the houses were recorded in the rate books. This prolonged construction period mirrored the slow pace of building on the rest of the estate, with the first Regent Square houses not finished until 1829 and Harrison Street still not complete in the 1830s. This was partly due to the continued operation of the brick kilns (by now surrounded by Sidmouth Mews) but the principal reason was almost certainly the housing bubble that developed from the end of the Napoleonic wars. This led to intense over-activity in the market and consequently an over-supply of houses, particularly those aimed at the wealthy, and a market crash in 1825. Even allowing for Payne's failings it is clear that he and the other builders were having great difficulty in promoting the Harrison Estate as a desirable locality, and perhaps explains the priority given to the cheaper houses of the Prospect Terrace area over the more expensive Regent Square.

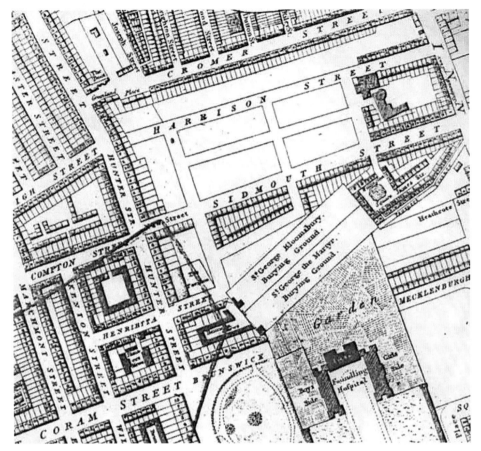

[4] Part of Horwood's map of London (1819 edition) showing the slow pace of development on the Harrison Estate. The Prospect Terrace area is largely complete. but only the south side of Regent Square appears to have houses; even these were unfinished. Surrounding estates, by contrast, are now almost entirely built up.

The completed development is best appreciated on the 1871 large-scale OS map [5], before the intervention of the School Board. The small patch of greenery in the centre of the square had by then gone.

14

[5] Cat's Meat Square on the 1:1056 scale Ordinance Survey map of 1871. Small alleys linked the south-west corner of the square with Prospect Terrace, and Sidmouth Street with Derry Street. Gates across Sidmouth Street and Heathcote Street tried to separate the area from 'respectable' Regent and Mecklenburgh Squares respectively.

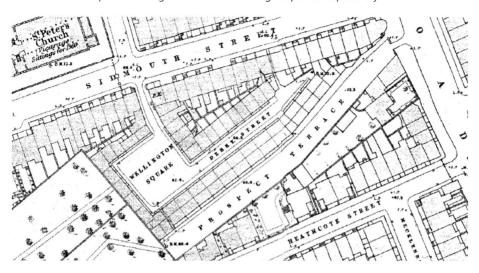

Notes, chapter 2

(CLSAC, Camden Local Studies and Archives Centre; LMA, London Metropolitan Archives; MDR, Middlesex Deeds Register; SPV, St Pancras Vestry)

1 Foundling Hospital Estate records, LMA. Quoted in Donald J Olsen, *Town Planning in London*, second edition 1982, p 84,

2 Ibid., p 88.

3 Ibid., p 90.

4 Act for paving and otherwise improving certain streets and other public passages… upon a certain piece of ground belonging to Thomas Harrison in St. Pancras. 50 Geo. III c. 170 (local). (*Survey of London*: volume 24)

5 MDR 1810/2/613 & 616, 1811/1/444, 446 & 448, 1811/4/600-604, LMA. (*The Survey of London*, Vol 24, Ch 5, The Harrison Estate, incorrectly gives the year 1818 for the first building leases in Harrison Street).

6 Several references to the brothers appear in the Harrison Estate Paving Commission minutes 1810-1815, LMA A/FH/E/05/001/001.

7 MDR 1810/2/615, LMA.

8 MDR 1810/2/614, LMA.

9 SPV Rate Books, 1812-24, CLSAC.

10 MDR/B/C/1810/059, LMA.

11 Harrison Estate Paving Commission minutes 1810-1815, LMA A/FH/E/05/001/001.

12 *London Gazette*, 6 April 1813, reprinted in *The Literary Panorama*, Vol 13.

13 *London Gazette*, 3 November 1812, reprinted in *Kentish Gazette*, 12 November 1812.

14 *The Times*, 8 October 1811.

15 *The Morning Post*, 10 March 1813.

16 He was buried on 31 October 1815 at St Pancras, "abode Wellington Square". St Pancras Parish Records, Ancestry.co.uk.

17 Will of James Payne of Prospect Terrace, 24 October 1815, National Archives, Prob 11/1574/ 321.

18 SPV Rate Books 1820s, CLSAC.

19 MDR 1819/2/743, LMA.

3 The Prospect Terrace back-to-backs: a London rarity
(Notes for this chapter on p 20)

London developed differently from the major industrial towns of the north; growth was more organic (but rapid) and the spread out from the centre was principally driven by the handsome returns to be made by building houses for the better off. Systematic development of housing for the skilled artisan classes was rare at the end of the 18th century, and for those below this level non-existent. Industry in the capital was small-scale; particular sectors, such as watch-making in Clerkenwell, were concentrated in small areas in an industrial ring surrounding the City. Housing tended to evolve out of necessity, with continual in-filling of yards and back gardens. As the century progressed, smaller houses for the shop-owning classes and better paid artisans became more widely available. Now (in 1810) Thomas Harrison chose to build a group of small houses that do not fit neatly into any contemporary category. Most unusually, he utilised the back-to-back terrace.

The back-to-back house should not be confused with terraces with small back yards separated from the back yards of the parallel street by an alley, sometimes erroneously called back-to-backs. Back-to-back houses actually shared a back wall. Rapid industrialisation in the north of England brought with it the need for large numbers of houses to be quickly and economically erected close to the new factories, mines and mills. They were usually two-storey, sometimes three, and built on 'green field' sites. As they had only one external wall and few windows, the terraces were cheap to build. The party walls were often only one brick thick.[1]

Such houses were almost unheard of in London, where the expansion from the centre was of a better class; workers' housing was concentrated in the already developed centre, within easy reach of work opportunities. This led to the proliferation of the infamous courts, whereby any space still available between properties was crammed full of small buildings, sometimes indeed without back elevations, but not in a purpose-built terrace. The courts were connected by a network of alleys, which emerged onto the main streets through openings often the size of doorways. Did Harrison intend his development to be something better than these courts for workers' families, or was he aiming it at a higher class of tenant?

Standards of housing and sanitation for the working class at the end of the Georgian period were much lower than those upheld by later social reformers. Privies were usually separate from houses, not sewer-drained and invariably shared. Timber-framed buildings were still commonplace. It is unlikely that Harrison's development would have been considered particularly inferior accommodation for artisans and servants. It is arguable that the square at least was aimed at a more comfortable class. The 1819 edition of Horwood's map of London ([4], p 14) still shows what appears to be a fenced-in grassed area in the middle of the square, a sign of respectability and certainly not something that would have been provided in any court or mews.

It was not till 1815 that Thomas Cubitt set up his builder's yard on the other side of Gray's Inn Road, so that Harrison would not have been aware in 1810 of potentially suitable tenants from Cubitt's workforce. Some of his workers did later reside in the development: the *Morning Chronicle* reported[2] in 1859 that Dennis Killard, a labourer living at No.14 James Street, who had been locked out of Cubitt's following a strike, then heckled men who had gone back to work. He was charged at Clerkenwell with being drunk and "annoying the workmen at Messrs Cubitt's" and fined 5s.[2] When Cubitt was giving evidence to a parliamentary commission in 1844 he was asked whether he had ever built a back-to-back house and he replied: "Never".[3] He did, however, defend their use, saying that "building them back-to-back is much cheaper, and if we were to prevent their being built back-to-back, we might in many cases prevent houses being built."

The adoption of the back-to-back model by Harrison and Payne was a response of sorts to a difficult site, which was hemmed in on two sides by the burial ground and its access road. With the hindsight of two centuries later, the whole model seems confused: the combination of an aspiring small square with adjacent poorly built housing ([4], p 14) was never going to form a respectable neighbourhood, just as the experienced Cockerell had predicted.

Photographs[4] by Henry Dixon and Son [6-8] show the housing stock that was used; these may be the only surviving images of a London back-to-back terrace. All the houses had three storeys plus basements and were broadly of the fourth rate in the Georgian order. Although by 1897 Wellington Square had been largely demolished for the Board School (opened in 1890), one house in it (No.15) is visible at the extreme left of [6] (p 18). The small first-floor balcony suggests that the houses on the Square sported the same plain façade as in Prospect Terrace ([7], p 19). Only one house in the whole development (No.13 Derry Street) had significant stucco ornamentation; it may once have been intended to be a public house. A Wellington Arms is mentioned in a newspaper report of 1846,[5] but this may have been the beer shop that certainly existed in one of the Wellington Square houses in the 1840s.

Prospect Terrace had some inconsistent use of stucco and the same tiny first-floor balconies as the Square. A crude attempt to distinguish No.8 (near the centre of the original terrace) by a different treatment of the façade is evident. Whatever attempt was being made to capitalise on the "prospect", this was by now fast disappearing as the Foundling and Calthorpe estates developed to the south.

The houses on the north side of James Street had a conventional internal layout. That the houses on the south side had no backs is not obvious at ground level, but the photograph of the roofs ([8], p 20) reveals how shallow the houses were: only 13-14 ft, the whole double terrace being some 27 ft deep. The top storey of

17

[6] Derry Street (formerly James Street) in 1897, taken from Prospect Terrace Board School, by then built on part of Wellington Square. The houses to the left were "conventional", those to the right were one room deep and back-to-back with Prospect Terrace.

the back-to-back terrace was a half-mansard on each side (separated by a central gutter) behind a brick parapet, with a ceiling height of around 6 ft. Given the poor upkeep of the properties, flooding of houses on both sides from the central gutter must have been a regular occurrence. Back-to-backs in the north of England invariably had pitched roofs. The height of ceilings and room proportions below varied, perhaps reflecting the staged nature of building and the involvement of different builders, particularly after Payne died.

The back-to-back houses had two rooms side by side on each floor, the larger one on the first floor being 100-120 sq ft in area and 8 ft in height. The smaller room accommodated a staircase at the back so narrow that two people could not pass, although the central entrance passage was relatively generous.[6] The chimney stacks and parapet lines followed no uniform pattern. Drainage was substandard,

18

[7] Prospect Terrace in 1897, looking towards Gray's Inn Road. Jutting out at the far end
is the confectionery shop at No.1 Sidmouth Street and beyond that Ampton Street.
Note the unmade roadway which remained in the ownership of the two churches.

having been laid too shallow, and the whole was built without an effective main
drain, so that the basements, containing privies and washhouses, were always damp.
Inadequate areas gave poor light to the basements, especially in James Street; some
were later enlarged.

Whatever Harrison's original intentions, by the 1820s it must have been obvious
that the development was of a depressed character in a district that was quickly
becoming less fashionable as the better off moved westwards. The whole area east
of Bloomsbury, St Pancras Ward 8 as it later became, suffered in this respect and
never went through a period of prosperity before it declined. While some of the
better streets and squares managed to cling on to a degree of gentility, the more
modest streets quickly went downhill socially. There were simply too many better-
class houses in London, and not enough houses for lesser mortals.

[8] The rooftops of the back-to-back terrace photographed in 1897. The right-hand side of the terrace is Prospect Terrace and the left Derry Street, the central gutter being over the party wall. The flank wall dates from 1888, when the first five houses were demolished to make way for the school. The taller houses in the background are the south side of Sidmouth Street.

The original rating assessments show that Wellington Square at £25 was considered the best accommodation, versus £15-18 for James Street and £18 for Prospect Terrace. By contrast, Sidmouth Street houses (the backs of which are visible in [8]) were rated at £80.[7] The slight social distinctions within Cat's Meat Square were maintained throughout most of its life. Prospect Terrace might have commanded a higher rating had the thorny issue of the roadway been resolved.

Notes, chapter 3

1 For a detailed discussion on the development of the back-to-back house see Burnett, John, *A Social History of Housing 1815-1985*, 2nd edn 1986, pp 70-77.

2 *The Morning Chronicle*, 14 September 1859.

3 *First Report of the Commissioners for Inquiring into the State of Large Towns and Populous Districts*, Vol 2, 1845, p 264.

4 Henry Dixon and Son, 1897. These photographs were probably commissioned by St Pancras Vestry (SPV) rather than the LCC. Henry Dixon died in 1893 and his son Thomas carried on the business.

5 *Lloyd's Weekly Newspaper*, 6 September 1846.

6 *The Standard*, 22 September 1885 and Report to SPV by Dr J F Sykes, 4 January 1905.

7 SPV Rate Books, 1812-20, CLSAC.

4 Comings and goings: the population 1810-1845

(Notes for this chapter on p 23)

Evidence for the population structure of the Prospect Terrace area is sketchy before the 1841 census, which provides the first reliable data for the origins of the inhabitants and their occupations besides the number living there. However, anecdotal evidence, coupled with samples from records of baptisms and marriages, can give an impression of earlier decades. The population was not purely artisan, and the Square did attract a middling class of person at first, although some appeared to be experiencing hard times and therefore ready to put up with the seemingly endless construction works. An 1821 will[1] of William Hinwood, of No.12 Prospect Terrace describes him as a "Gentleman". A former assistant collector of taxes to the Skinners' Estate lived at No.16 Wellington Square in 1825.[2] Besides James Payne and Bennett, another bankrupt is listed[3] in 1817 as a merchant of Wellington Square.

A strange case of 1815 concerning the alleged imprisonment of a French woman at No.12 Wellington Square was reported in *The Times*.[4] A Mr Bindon, described as an attorney, and his wife were accused of befriending the woman (said to be 'possessed of considerable property') and taking her to their house where she was 'confined and treated as a lunatic'. She was eventually rescued and taken to the house of a 'respectable man' in Wellington Place. The tone of the report, with its references to the 'neighbours of Wellington Square', suggests respectability.

From birth and marriage records, the social group that stands out consistently in the 1820s and early 1830s is people in domestic service. Artisans of various occupations are present but servants, grooms, coachmen and the like are the most numerous. Earlier, an advertisement in the *Morning Post* in 1816 placed by a 'respectable young women' of 8 Prospect Terrace sought a position as housemaid in a 'genteel regular family'.[5] In 1817 a 'Young Woman who can work at her needle' of 8 James Street was looking for a placement as an 'Attendant on an elderly Lady'.[6] Advertisements of this sort gradually dwindled in the 1830s. It cannot of course be established whether servants were using the streets as lodgings between placements or whether they served local households.

In 1823 James William Simpson was apprehended at his lodgings at No.12 James Street. He had been dismissed from his post as a footman to the Marchioness of Londonderry and thereafter had stolen a large quantity of goods and clothes from her New Forest estate. An officer from Bow Street tracked him down at night and described the area as 'obscure, intricate and badly lighted'.[7] Reports of crime in the Prospect Terrace area are actually very rare before 1840.

One servant living in Wellington Square in 1833 was 'William, An African', about 27 years old. He was baptised at St Peter's Regent Square on 17 March; written across the spaces for the parents' names are the words "a slave", and below that "Antonio is his surname".[8] The Slavery Abolition Act was passed a few months later and in 1841 he was in service to a merchant in Upper Bedford Place.

John Smith, an attorney's clerk, lived at No.13 and then No.16 Wellington Square[8] in the 1820s; he appears to be one of the first resident landlords of several properties, for by the end of the decade he had acquired the sub-leases of other houses – by 1840 he had a portfolio of 11 houses.[9] His first wife was probably the Mary Smith of Wellington Square who died in 1852, described in 1851 as a "Proprietor of houses". John Smith died on 15 April 1861 leaving £800 in his estate[10], but had by then moved to Croydon with a presumed second wife, Martha. The subsequent ownership structure in the Prospect Terrace area will be examined in more detail later, but the advent of landlords of this type points to the increasing use of the houses for lodgings and their concomitant division into a number of households. By the end of the 1820s, few of the houses were likely to be used for single-family occupation.

In 1831 90% of the population of London still lived within the old City boundaries but over the next decade the population grew rapidly and with nearly the whole district now built up, south St Pancras started to take on the air of a Metropolitan area. The very poor were still concentrated in the old industrial ring surrounding the City, such as Farringdon and parts of Holborn. Until the 1840s, south St Pancras generally would not have been regarded as especially impoverished, certainly not compared with areas such as Farringdon or St Giles.

The 1841 census records a total of 659 people in 176 households in the Prospect Terrace area.[11] As there were 56 houses here with approximately 330 rooms (excluding basements) this gives an average density of 2 persons per room, or just under 12 per house. The average per house in London was just over 7 at this time and in St Pancras 8.5. In the more established slums of Westminster and St Giles, however, average densities of 24 per house were recorded by Edwin Chadwick in 1841.[12]

Of the heads of these households, 79 were born in Middlesex, and 33 (18.8%) were Irish-born. The Irish residents were not recent arrivals: from the ages of many of their children born in the county it is clear that they were principally immigrants from the 1820s. Of the Irish households, 18 were in James Street and only three in Prospect Terrace. This, together with the frequency of occupations such as labourers in the former, provides evidence that James Street was by the 1840s almost entirely given over to lodgings. Prospect Terrace also had its fair share of lodging houses: in 1840 a fire at Mr Rankin's, No.9 Prospect Terrace 'destroyed the whole of the premises and furniture which unfortunately belonged to poor lodgers'.[13] An 1842 case of the theft of an apple from a chandler's shop in Wellington Place by a boy living with his destitute family in a room in Wellington Square also demonstrates that poverty was established in the area. The boy was sent to sea and the mother awarded £2 from the poor fund.[14]

There is an evident decline in service occupations by 1841 and a sizeable contingent of artisan trades, particular amongst those recorded as born "out of county". But in Wellington Square there are still a few clerks, policemen and traders, and in 1844 a charge of assaulting his wife was brought against 'Richard James Chapman, a respectable-looking, middle aged man, residing at No.7 Wellington Square, an actor at Drury Lane Theatre'.[15] By 1845 the demographic trends were well established and the Prospect Terrace area could go in only one direction.

Notes, chapter 4

1 Will of William Hinwood of Prospect Terrace, 16 February 1821, National Archives Prob 11/1647/104.

2 St Pancras Church Baptism records, 1825, Ancestry.co.uk.

3 *London Gazette*, 21 January 1817.

4 *The Times*, 17 July 1815.

5 *The Morning Post*, 23 November 1816.

6 Ibid, 18 February 1817.

7 *Royal Cornwall Gazette*, 11 January 1823

8 St Peter's Regent Square baptism register, 17 March 1833, Ancestry.co.uk.

9 SPV Rate Books 1824-41, CLSAC.

10 National Probate Calendar (Index of Wills and Administrations), 1861-1941, Ancestry.co.uk.

11 1841 England Census, National Archives, Ancestry.co.uk.

12 Wohl, Anthony S, *The Eternal Slum*, 1977, 2nd edn, pp 22-23.

13 *Morning Chronicle*, 28 December 1840.

14 *The Standard*, 19 January 1842.

15 *Lloyds Weekly Newspaper*, 13 October 1844.

5 The Cockney Irish in Cat's Meat Square: social decline 1845-1885

(Notes for this chapter on p 32)

On a Sunday morning in September 1885 a reporter on *The Standard* newspaper joined one of the St Pancras Vestry sanitary inspectors on his rounds, taking in Prospect Terrace, the Cromer Street courts and Poplar Place. On reaching the latter he writes: "For the first time during the morning someone wants to beg. It is needless to say the woman is Irish. The unnecessary dirt would proclaim that quite as well as her brogue. The Cockney Irish, so my companion tells me, seem to have the dirty habits of the Irish and the English added together".[1]

Such was the widespread view of Irish people that held sway over the 19th century and indeed persisted well into the 20th. Apart from outright hostility to Irish-born people, there developed the concept of the "Cockney Irish", to include anyone from the poor who had Irish heritage or who had married an Irish man or woman. This allowed Cat's Meat Square and other Ward 8 rookeries to be labelled 'Irish' for much, if not all, of their existence. Even in the last days of Derry Street, Mary Ward and her volunteers at the Passmore Edwards Settlement were still describing the children as 'mostly Irish'.[2] But was this actually the case? The 1841 census indeed showed Irish people making up a significant proportion of the population but did this increase over the rest of the century?

The mid-1840s saw the start of a sustained rise in the population of London. Housing pressures increased hugely and the lowest classes began to be displaced from the centre of London. Peripheral areas such as south St Pancras were in the front of the firing line and the housing crisis of the 1880s was the inevitable result.

The Great Famine in Ireland in the mid-1840s led to a surge in Irish migration into London, much of it from very poor rural communities in the south west. Inevitably, many of these arrivals would head to areas already containing sizable populations of people of Irish origin such as St Giles and the area around Saffron Hill. Here was also the cheapest accommodation. Unfortunately, this period also saw the authorities commence wholesale clearances of insanitary neighbourhoods such as the Fleet Valley. New Oxford Street was driven through the heart of the St Giles rookery in 1844-47. The rising numbers entering London, whether from Ireland of other parts of the UK, were joined by those evicted from these poor areas in the competition for living space as near as possible to work opportunities.

By 1851 the population of the Prospect Terrace area had increased to 739, a rise of 12% over 10 years.[3] Irish-headed households had increased from 33 to 50 (23.5% of the total), but there was also a similar increase in householders from outside London and Middlesex. There is no evidence that the area was infamous then. Press reports from the 1850s rarely mention poverty, though one reports the death of 'Mary Devereu, aged 49, the wife of an Irish hawker, living at 18 James Street'.[4] Henry Mayhew, in references to the Gray's Inn Lane district, does not mention

Prospect Terrace but lists Cromer Street (one street north of Harrison Street) as being an established and 'thickly populated' Irish area.[5]

From 1855, the Metropolis Local Management Act obliged London vestries to appoint and publish annual reports from a Medical Officer of Health on sanitary conditions in their parishes. Dr Thomas Hillier, the first holder of the post in St Pancras, and a distinguished physician at the children's hospital at Great Ormond Street, listed Wellington Square and James Street under areas with poor drainage in his initial report,[6] but by his third report in 1858 he clearly had grave concerns about the very high mortality rates locally. Specifically, he listed James Street and Wellington Square (43 and 33 deaths per 1,000 population respectively), a number of the Cromer Street courts (Melina Place, 50 per 1,000, being the worst) and Poplar Place (behind Hunter Street Police Station, 79 per 1,000), together with Colonnade and others. Prospect Terrace itself had a relatively unremarkable death rate of 18 in that year (the London average was 23), and Mecklenburgh Square the best one at 9 per 1,000.[7]

So by the 1850s Cat's Meat Square was recognised, in some circles at least, as an insanitary area. To some extent the lower standards of 1810 and the poor construction of the houses meant it had always been so, but its real decline probably dated from the early 1830s with the systematic subdivision of the houses by landlords such as John Smith, and accelerated rapidly in the 1840s. Some of the Cromer Street courts were undoubtedly worse. This set of small streets and courts ran north of Cromer Street to North Place or Terrace (now Argyle Walk) ([9], p 26) The significant number of Irish people here very probably also dates from the early 1830s, but just under 25% was to mark the high point of the number of Irish households in Prospect Terrace. From 1851 onwards there was a steady decline, and this was true across London, but as years went by the place of new births would be recorded as London or Middlesex, so that the numbers with Irish heritage would have continued to rise. Hence the 'Irish Colony' tag persisted for many decades.

In 1861 the population had risen by another 10% to 813, with a small decline in the number of Irish-born households.[8] Average room occupancy had increased to 2.4 persons. Thomas Hillier continued to push for vestry action on drainage and stated in his report of 1862 that in James Street in 1861: 'the deaths under 5 years of age in this year amounted to 330 per thousand of the number living at that age. The number of deaths at all ages in James Street amounted to 16 which gives the enormously high death rate of 54 per thousand....In this street there are underground kitchens occupied as dwelling rooms imperfectly drained, owing to a sewer of insufficient depth; each room is occupied by a family, and in some of the houses the tops of the staircases are not supplied with the means of ventilation; the inhabitants are poor and some of them intemperate'. In Wellington Square, Hillier

[9] The Cromer Street area in 1871. The small streets and courts running north of Cromer Street developed as cul-de-sacs as they hit the boundary with the Battle Bridge Estate. One of the worst, tiny Melina Place ran east off the top of Riley Street and was owned by a St Pancras Vestryman.

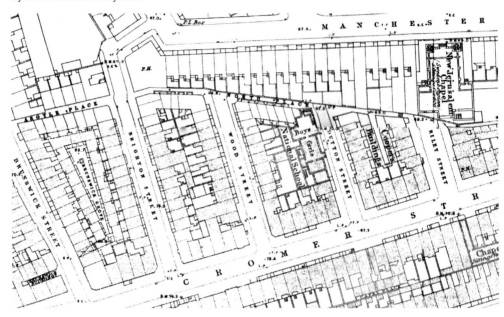

notes that 'there has been nearly as high a mortality (and) the same evils exist; both the paving and drainage of this square call for improvement'.[9]

Hillier went on to say that Poplar Place had had an average death rate of 34 per thousand over the preceding six years and is 'occupied by the Irish whose habits are most dirty and their mode of living most irregular'.[9] What the irregularity was is not clear but Hillier conveniently ignores the desperate poverty of these people as a direct contributor to their housing conditions. Poplar Place (and Compton Place with which it was linked) [10] had been built in 1809. Previously stables, the housing was put up in the typical court method by George Payne. It quickly degenerated and may well be called south St Pancras' first slum – in 1823 the residents of Compton Street were already complaining 'that great riots have been committed by the inhabitants of Compton Place (who are chiefly Irish)'.[10] Various attempts were made by the Foundling Estate to improve the property over the years (including leasing part of it to build a police station) but it continued on a downward path.

Hillier's efforts were mainly directed at getting the vestry to improve the sewers, and the cholera outbreaks of the 1850s and 60s provided the spur for increased action. The owners of the insanitary houses were not the principal target, but as will be seen later, the vestry was itself a constant frustration to successive medical officers. Indeed the vestry passed a resolution 'expressly forbidding' Hillier to attend vestry meetings except at their request.[11] Opposition to Hillier on the vestry was often led by a fellow medical man, Dr William Collins, who accused him of trying to bring the vestry into contempt. Collins was also a vociferous campaigner against

26

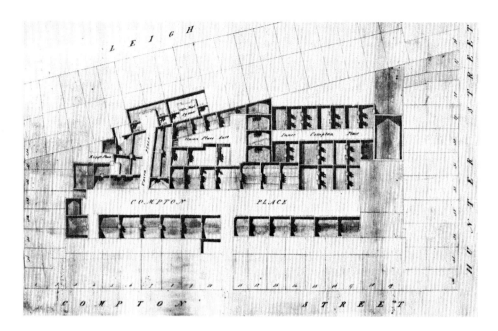

[10] Plan of Compton Place and neighbouring courts, c.1809. It was later generally known as Poplar Place. Both Joseph Kay of the Foundling Estate and Thomas Hillier called for its demolition in the 1850s. Most of the houses were finally cleared away in December 1885.

vaccination (his son Sir William Job Collins later became a St Pancras MP). When Hillier proposed that the vestry appoint two additional sanitary inspectors Collins said it 'ought to be treated with the contempt it deserved'.[12] Dr Hillier died in 1868 and the *British Medical Journal* noted that 'his unwearied labours' as medical officer for the vestry was 'ill repaid by its authorities'.[13] He was succeeded by Dr (later Sir) Thomas Stevenson, a noted toxicologist.

When in the mid-1860s the Metropolitan Board of Works comprehensively overhauled London's street names to reduce the number of streets bearing the same name, especially those linked to royalty, James Street became Derry Street.[14] For probably the same reason nearby George Street was renamed Wicklow Street: a local Irish theme seems to have been the aim.

In 1871 the Central Middlesex coroner heard the case of the death of 5-month-old William Tann, the illegitimate son of a 19-year-old woman living in the attic of No.2 Derry Street with her younger sister and another child. The mother was 'obliged to leave home at five o'clock in the morning and did not return home until late in the evening' in order to work at a white lead factory in Kingsland, for which she was paid 9s a week. The toxic nature of the work made her constantly ill. The cause of death was starvation 'accelerated by want of proper food'. The court was told that the mother was refused poor relief as she was able-bodied and from her wages she paid 1s 9d a week rent for the room, leaving 7s 3d to support a family of four.[15] 'This is a most important case and one which it would do well for society to hear of and act upon' said the coroner.[16] 'Such is life; and death in life, in Derry

27

Street, Gray's Inn Road' remarked the *Birmingham Daily Post*.[17]

Increasingly, these were the real conditions of the inhabitants of areas such as Cat's Meat Square. The high death rates were just as likely to be caused by absolute poverty as from problems with drainage and ventilation, which had increasingly become the focus of social reformers, who tended to play down the role of very low wages and casualisation and blame physical housing defects and intemperate inhabitants. But the economic downturns of the late 1870s and 80s were to exacerbate the poverty and with it the housing crisis.

The census of 1871 showed a rise in the Prospect Terrace population to 886, with a room density of 2.6 and an average of 16.4 people per house.[18] These average figures include single lodgers and couples; overcrowding for families was certainly worse, with five or more to a room now common. The single largest pressure on south St Pancras since the last census had been the clearance of Agar Town for the Midland Railway and the resultant eviction of thousands of people (though Agar Town never appears as a birthplace in any census of Prospect Terrace). The MBW's street improvement programme, which included the widening of Gray's Inn Road and Theobalds Road, was also in full swing and in central London poor housing was being demolished to make way for new offices and warehouses: a growing number of inhabitants in Cat's Meat Square gave their place of birth as Clerkenwell, Westminster, the Strand and other central districts.

Dr Stevenson submitted a report to the St Pancras Vestry in 1876 suggesting the possible application of the 1875 Artisans and Labourers' Dwellings Act.[19] Tensions were again emerging between the Medical Officer's attempts to deal with rising overcrowding and the reluctance of the St Pancras Vestry to act. After stating that 1875 was on the whole a relatively healthy year, Stevenson goes on to say: 'In one street (Derry Street, Ward 8) I found an unusual rate of mortality....There were the most glaring yet ordinary Sanitary defects in these houses which are of defective construction. The powers of the Nuisances Removal Acts have been put in force. If these are found insufficient it may be necessary to declare this an unhealthy district within the meaning of the Statute of 1875.'

The 1875 Act (generally known as the Cross Act, after Richard Cross, the Home Secretary) permitted vestries to petition the MBW to buy up slum areas with compensation for the owners. The land was usually sold to philanthropic housing societies. In fact, the St Pancras insanitary areas were generally too small for the Act to apply. Torrens' Act of 1868 had made similar provisions for vestries to acquire smaller sites, without compensation, but it was difficult to implement, and as there was no obligation on vestries to build replacement housing, demolitions simply led to more overcrowding. Far from using this or any other legislation, the vestry was more interested in putting obstacles in the way of

28

Dr Stevenson's efforts. His intension had been to provide a comprehensive review of insanitary areas 'but this design has been frustrated'. Stevenson's proposals for the deployment of what few sanitary inspectors there were had been overruled by the vestry Sanitary Committee, and 'the only Inspector of mature experience in detailed house inspection is removed from the sphere', to another district.[19] Stevenson threatened to resign over the number of sanitary inspectors and finally did so in 1878. Dr Shirley Foster Murphy replaced him and within a few years matters would come to a head.

One of his earlier challenges in the post was the unusual case of the private dissecting room in the former St George the Martyr burial ground (closed to burials in 1856). A Dr Thomas Cooke had set up the dissecting room in 1877 for the instruction of medical students. By 1880 residents in the surrounding streets were complaining of 'most unpleasant smells'[20] from the burning of sawdust and refuse at the Wellington Square end of the burial ground. A 'gentleman from Wellington Square'[21] (probably one of the landlords) was said to have taken a prominent part in the complaints to the vestry Sanitary Committee and he alleged that illness and mortality had increased since the room's creation. Of course, the increase was more likely to be the result of overcrowding in the houses. Dr Murphy discovered a variety of animal refuse (including four dead cats) in the overgrown and dilapidated burial ground. The complaints were dismissed and the dissecting room was permitted to remain open following some improvements to drainage.

As the 1880s dawned, Cat's Meat Square was increasingly seen as one of St Pancras' worst slums ([11], p 30). The census of 1881 showed[22] an increase in inhabitants to 907 (despite two houses being empty, probably due to periodic closure orders). This decade was to mark the high point for absolute numbers, as the Board School demolitions were to take place towards the end of it. Irish-born households had declined to 42 (16%) and two-thirds of household heads now gave their place of birth as within the putative County of London boundary. Yet it was still being described as 'a colony of Irish residing in Prospect Place and Wellington Square' and 'a squalid and over-crowded locality (with) a great number of young Irish Labourers'.[23]

The Times reported an explosion in the basement of No.8 Derry Street in 1882, which provoked immediate panic that the house was being used for 'the storage of large quantities of Fenian ammunition'.[24] In fact it was caused by the detonation of defective cartridges hidden behind the copper and up the chimney by a young woman worker at Eley's Cartridge Manufactory, in Gray's Inn Road. Eley's employed many factory girls from Derry Street and this one, terrified that her poor work would be discovered, secreted as many as 250 cartridges in and around the little-used copper. Unfortunately a charwoman, Mrs Booth, chose to do some washing late at

[11] Prospect Terrace in 1904, but little changed from the 1870s. The wall to the left marked the boundary with the Foundling Estate, which had been keen to shut out the view to the 'inferior and irregular buildings' of Prospect Terrace.

night; she escaped serious injury in the ensuing explosion. The *Freeman's Journal* reported that 300 police had surrounded the area and kept the residents, 'the poorest class of Irishmen', out on the street for two hours in the middle of the night.[25] Already poor relations between the police and the inhabitants were said to have worsened as a result of the incident.

On 30 January 1882, the case of William Mason aged 66 of No.13 Prospect Terrace gave an indication into the thinking of Dr Murphy and the St Pancras sanitary department. The coroner's court heard that Mr Moon, one of the St Pancras Workhouse relieving officers, was called to Prospect Terrace and found Mason dead on the floor of a room 'more like a pigsty than a habitation for human beings'.[26] The man, his wife and his married daughter, her husband and their two children all slept in the small room of 600 cu ft for which they paid 3s 6d rent and 'he had evidently undergone dreadful privation'. William Rouch, the Chief Sanitary Inspector, said he felt it was his duty to serve the landlord with a notice to prevent continued overcrowding, for although the condition of the house was 'fairly good, he believed every room in it was overcrowded'.

Rouch outlined how there was power open to vestries under the 1866 Sanitary Act to compel the registration of all houses let out in tenements, which would set the maximum number allowed to occupy each room. The coroner was 'glad to hear such an old and experienced officer as Mr Inspector Rouch express himself as he had done, when for such places as this exorbitant rents were levied upon the poor by extortionate landlords'.[26] Increasingly Medical Officers of Health and their inspectors were suggesting the use of the Sanitary Act as a way of mitigating overcrowding without wholesale evictions and clearances, although the tactic was comprehensively employed by only two London vestries, Hackney and Chelsea. As was to become clear, a large number of vestries, including St Pancras, resisted the use of the Act, claiming it would increase homelessness – but of course it would be to the detriment of landlords, as the income per house would be slashed.

By the mid-1880s Cat's Meat Square had reached a low point and little had been done to stem the rise in overcrowding and poverty. But why was it called Cat's Meat Square?

Notes, chapter 5

1 *The Standard*,
22 September 1885.

2 *The Times*,
5 February 1906.

3 1851 England Census,
National Archives (Ancestry.
co.uk).

4 *Lloyds Weekly Newspaper*,
7 December 1851.

5 Mayhew, Henry, *London
Labour and the London Poor*,
1851, Vol 1, p 109.

6 First Annual Report of the
Medical Officer of Health,
SPV, 1856, p 12
(CLSAC).

7 Third Annual Report of the
Medical Officer of Health,
SPV, 1858, pp 4-6
(CLSAC).

8 1861 England Census,
National Archives
(Ancestry.co.uk).

9 Seventh Annual Report
of the Medical Officer
of Health, SPV, 1862,
p 4 (CLSAC).

10 Olsen, Donald J, *Town
Planning in London*,
2nd edn 1982, p 130.

11 Date unknown.
Reported in *The Times*,
11 January 1867.

12 *Marylebone Mercury*,
24 February 1866.

13 *British Medical Journal*,
14 November 1868
(bound volume 2, p 529).

14 SPV Rate Books 1865
(CLSAC).

15 *Reynolds Newspaper*,
24 September 1871.

16 *Lloyd's Weekly Newspaper*,
24 September 1871.

17 *Birmingham Daily Post*,
21 September 1871.

18 1871 England Census,
National Archives
(Ancestry.co.uk).

19 Medical Officer's Report
... on the Artizans and
Labourers' Dwellings Act,
24 March 1876,
SPV records (CLSAC).

20 *The Manchester Courier*,
17 July 1880.

21 SPV Sanitary
Committee minutes,
28 July 1880 (CLSAC).

22 1881 England Census,
National Archives
(Ancestry.co.uk).

23 *The Times*,
3 September 1881.

24 *The Times*,
17 July 1882.

25 *The Freeman's Journal*,
17 July 1882.

26 *The Times*,
31 January 1882.

On 14 January 1877, an inquest was heard into the death of Mary Newton, aged 50, whose 'frightfully emaciated' body was found in the back parlour of No.5 Derry Street. *Reynold's Newspaper* reported that Derry Street was part of 'Wellington – or as it is more generally known from its character as a rookery, "Cat's-meat" – Square'. The court was told that 'the whole of the houses in this Cat's-meat-square are in a filthy and unsanitary condition'.[1] This is the first recorded reference to Cat's Meat Square, but it implies that the name had been in use for some time. Five years later saw a further reference when *Reynold's News* reported that the coroner had received information on the death of 63-year-old Thomas Morrice in 'distressing circumstances at No.8 Derry Street, Wellington Square, otherwise Cat's-meat-square'.[2]

At an inquest held in July 1887, the wife of Soloman Worms, a bricklayer's labourer, was giving evidence into her husband's death by a falling wall in Cromer Street. On stating her address as No.11 Wellington Square, "properly called Cat's-meat-square", a laugh went round the courtroom.[3] Cat's Meat Square appears therefore to have been in use in some circles for at least the last quarter of the 19th century. Despite frequent mentions of the whole area in official papers and the press, the Cat's Meat tag does not appear with any regularity, so that its use seems to have been fairly localised.

No further references appear until January 1900, when another coroner's case received more widespread press attention. Under the headline EIGHT IN ONE ROOM, the *Daily News* reported on the death from consumption of 2-year-old Rose Walters at No.14 Wellington Square. A juror helpfully pointed out that 'Wellington-place forms part of what is known as "Cat's Meat-square". It is near Regent's-square and has been a plague spot for years. It is condemned as an insanitary area.'[4] The *Pall Mall Gazette* repeated the details of the case[5] in 'the district poetically known as "Cat's Meat-square"'. The reference to poetry clearly had an effect, for within a week *Punch* had published an anonymous poem[6] called Cat's Meat Square which concluded:

> "Air ! Give us air !
> Away with these fever-dens ! Sweep them away
> With the pitiless Harpies that batten and prey
> On Cat's Meat Square !"

Six weeks later, on 24 February 1900, the long-running Oxford journal *Notes and Queries* published a question on Cat's Meat Square from one 'Tabitha': "I have been told that this fictitious name was given by Dickens to a notoriously insanitary neighbourhood, but can find no mention of it in his novels. Could any contributor kindly help me?" The only reply simply pointed to the inquest reports and that the area is 'known locally today as "Cat's-Meat Square"'.[7] The reference to Dickens is intriguing, for the name does have a Dickensian ring to it. He must have known the area well, it being a mere 10-minute stroll from Doughty Street through Mecklenburgh Square. But there is no evidence that the name was in use in the 1830s when Dickens lived there, and nothing has emerged from his writings. At that stage in its history, the Prospect Terrace area was also not especially poor and could not yet be described as a rookery, although it was on a downward trajectory when Dickens left Doughty Street in 1839.

Certainly a local name, then, but why Cat's Meat? There is no reference to the cat's meat trade in any census from 1841 onwards, but numerous costermongers and hawkers appear over the decades and these more generic terms may well have included cat's meat sellers [12], who typically sold boiled horse meat from barrows.

Gray's Inn Lane was well known for horse boilers according to one account[8] and was 'notorious for the supply of cat's meat'. Nearby Smithfield was another centre for the horse meat trade and north of King's Cross, in so-called Belle Isle, stood one of London's largest horse slaughterers, where 'many tons of nutriment for the feline species are daily boiled in the immense coppers and carried away every morning by a legion of industrious barrowmen'.[9]

So it is possible that the name of a noxious trade was linked to an insanitary area or that its residents did include a significant number of cat's meat sellers, although Henry Mayhew at least considered cat's meat sellers to be relatively well off compared to most hawkers.[10] But another view from 1868 said[11] that 'this branch of street trade numbers among it men, whose sole worldly possession is the miserable basket, in which they carry their merchandise, and women, who can just manage to crawl along from house to house with their scanty baskets of horseflesh'. The alternative notion that the inhabitants of Cat's Meat Square were so destitute that they resorted to eating horse meat is unlikely, the cultural aversion being too strong and 'the odour arising from it is so disagreeable'.[11]

Perhaps the best clue is the statement in the first recorded reference[1] in 1877 in which Wellington Square and its streets were 'more generally known from its *character as a rookery*' as Cat's Meat Square. In all probability it was a denigrating nickname applied by a witty local. Its real origin may never be known.

[12] A Cat's Meat Man in East London, c.1901. Detail of photograph by John Galt.

Notes, chapter 6

1 *Reynold's Newspaper*, 14 January 1877.

2 Ibid., 14 May 1882.

3 *Illustrated Police News*, 30 July 1887.

4 *Daily News*, 3 January 1900.

5 *Pall Mall Gazette*, 3 January 1900.

6 *Punch*, 10 January 1900.

7 *Notes and Queries*, 24 February 1900.

8 *Streetology of London*, ed. Jack Rag, 1837, p 25.

9 Greenwood, James, *In strange company*, 2nd edn, 1874, ch.7.

10 Mayhew, Henry, *London Labour and the London Poor*, Vol 1, p 183.

11 Article by W Baird in *Chatterbox*, 1868 (Historium.com).

To understand the ownership structure of Cat's Meat Square and of the other south St Pancras slum areas one must start with the leasehold system underpinning property ownership in 19th-century London. Estate owners like the Harrisons rarely sold the freehold of their developments, instead granting building leases which yielded income from ground rents. In theory, covenants in the leases would prevent dilapidations, and the obligations of the head lease cascaded down through any subleasing that might, and all too frequently did, take place. The original leases were typically for 99 years, subleases much less, often as little as 7 years. Subletting would extend right down to a tenant with two rooms who rented one out. A labyrinthine structure developed which is very hard to penetrate, as records for the lower end of the market are rarely available. The system was exploited very successfully by the small-scale property owners of the period, particularly in the 1870s and 80s when investing in tenement houses became popular with small traders, builders and shop keepers – who were also typical of the membership of London vestries, and often known collectively as the "shopocracy".

Harry Lawson, Liberal MP for St Pancras West from 1885 to 1892 summed up the workings of this structure in a speech[1] in the House of Commons in May 1889:

'At the point when this rickety tenure is about to break down at the fag end of the lease, you bring into play the house jobber, or house farmer, of the type of the notorious Mr Flight, who gets a great number of houses into his hands, and then sweats extortionate rents out of his luckless tenants. The practice is to do little or nothing to mend the unsanitary and dilapidated condition of the house. A coat of whitewash covers a multitude of sins. It may be said that by the covenants of the lease lessees are forced to keep [the property] in good repair. Unfortunately, those covenants have neither been fulfilled nor enforced.'

In 1884 the Royal Commission on the Housing of the Working Classes (RCHWC), in taking evidence on the Prospect Terrace area, was to hear that a 'great deal of property in this neighbourhood, I believe, although I could not say of my knowledge, belongs to a Mrs Flight',[2] and the index to the evidence states that Flight is the 'landlord of Prospect Terrace houses'.[3] Thomas Flight was born in 1791, a grandson of Thomas Flight of Royal Worcester porcelain fame. A man with fingers in many pies, his business interests were based in Bond Court in Walbrook, home of many City merchants. He had substantial houses in Norwood and Brighton and for a time owned Laycock's Dairy in Islington, one of London's largest. Flight was also well known as a moneylender, frequently pursuing his 'clients' through the courts.

From the middle of the century, he was by far the biggest and most notorious of the London slum property owners, with 18,000 houses[4] in virtually every poor area of the capital. The Lady Correspondent of the *Daily Telegraph* wrote that 'There are long lines of tenements in every low part of London which bring in to their owner, a certain Mr Flight, a man possessed of enormous wealth, an annual income which puts that of many a foreign potentate to shame'.[5] He died in 1877 and his wife Matilda continued to profit from their property empire until her death in 1900. The Flights alone probably housed as many people as did all the philanthropic housing societies, whose rooms had reached an estimated 123,000 by 1905. The Flights were, though, quite unlike the typical small house farmer of the time.

Whether Flight acquired any of Prospect Terrace it is difficult to say, because he used such devious methods. He would frequently buy up leases in the name of his clerks, keeping control of the property by virtue of having advanced the mortgage. He sublet his quarterly rented property to a small landlord and therefore did not appear in rate books. His name does occur in rate books for property rented weekly directly to tenants, for instance the Cromer Street courts, and in 1872 he appears as the owner of houses in North Place, Wood Street, all of Brunswick Grove and virtually all of the improbably-named Peace Cottages.[6] In the 1880s they were in the name of Matilda Flight.[7]

Octavia Hill tried on occasions to get 'that man Flight' to sell properties to her to renovate under her improvement schemes, but he always refused.[8] Arrears of rent (either by small landlords or tenants) would see the tenants and their possessions thrown out on the street by Flight's men. St Pancras Vestry minutes of March 1870 refer to a public meeting held in Somers Town against evictions organised by Flight.[9] By 1885, the Flight's holdings around Cromer Street were threatened by clearances and Matilda Flight attempted to extract compensation from St Pancras Vestry under the Cross Act. The request was declined as 'she is not an owner within the meaning of the Act'.[10] It is likely that the local small property owners and their friends on the vestry did not have much time for the likes of Thomas and Matilda Flight, who were in a different league altogether.

If Flight was a leaseholder in Cat's Meat Square, it is not clear who he was leasing from or to. He did have the opportunity to buy the freehold of the Regent Square development in 1844 when the whole was put on the market.[11] The reason for the sale, and the outcome, is uncertain but the Harrison Estate seems to have kept control. Flight certainly was not the end lessee or ratepayer, he may have been a middleman and he was undoubtedly an important landlord in St Pancras, but the evidence for his presence in Prospect Terrace is unconvincing. We can, however, identify some of the owners in the latter half of the century, and particularly two who were also St Pancras Vestrymen.

George Gordon was born around 1826 in County Tyrone and was a house painter by trade. He first appears in 1851 in a lodging house in Somers Town but by the 1861 census he is a lodger, and still described as a house painter, with Frederick and Catherine Garbit at No.1 Mecklenburgh Terrace, Gray's Inn Road, a respectable address.[12] Events then took a bizarre turn when Frederick was convicted of bigamy in September 1863 and sentenced to 6 months' imprisonment, pleading in mitigation that he had been deserted by Catherine who had 'grossly misconducted herself'.[13] Catherine Garbit filed for divorce in the same year[14] and in 1865 married George Gordon at Holy Trinity, Gray's Inn Road.[15] As church weddings by divorcees were not permitted, subterfuge was evidently employed. In 1871 they were at the same address (then known as No.207 Gray's Inn Road) with seven children from the two marriages. Gordon was now described as a house agent.[16] This was because a lease of March 1862[17] had assigned a number of houses in Prospect Terrace and Wellington Square to Gordon from the estate of one John Smith, who had died the previous year (p 22). By 1866 he had seven houses in each locality.[18] George Gordon clearly had the funds to buy the property in 1862 (a year after being a lowly lodger and house painter), and it must have come from the Garbits in some way, with or without Frederick's blessing.

George Gordon certainly knew what he was buying into – the Prospect Terrace area was then well on the way to becoming overcrowded and insanitary – but Gordon had plans. In 1869 he was elected to the St Pancras Vestry,[19] almost certainly by a show of hands, and he was to remain a member until 1885. He picked up houses in Cromer Street and the small streets and courts running off it and in the 1860s he constantly appealed against the rating assessments of his property. In a rare appearance at an inquest in December 1876 he is described[20] as a vestryman and collector of rents; it transpired that he was charging 2s rent for a room in Cromer Street from an old woman living on poor relief consisting of '3s and a loaf'. He was also acting as agent for a number of owners of one or two houses and was the most significant and powerful figure in Cat's Meat Square for 40 years, virtually up until its demolition in 1906.

Gordon does not appear to have been particularly active in the vestry, preferring simply to cultivate a circle of influential friends in order to deter unwelcome meddling from the Medical Officer and his inspectors. As overcrowding and rents rose, Gordon prospered. By 1884 he had moved with his family to Aubrey Villa, Torrington Park in then semi-rural North Finchley.[21] He established an office in the front left parlour of No.7 Prospect Terrace: the words 'Gordon Office' can just be made out in the window on the 1897 photograph [13]. The man standing in the doorway may be Gordon himself. The office also allowed Gordon to qualify as a holder of rateable property and thus retain vestry and voting rights in St Pancras.

What the tenants of his properties thought of him can only be guessed at. He was not popular with the liberal-leaning St Pancras Guardian, which wrote in January 1885: 'Mr Gordon is a lucky man....Mr Gordon is the happy possessor of a number of houses which the vestry inspectors consider unfit for habitation unless certain

improvements and alterations are made in them – alterations and improvements that would necessitate an exceedingly large outlay'.[22] But as the School Board wanted to buy part of the site, Gordon went before the Sanitary Committee to ask for a delay in improvement notices. The Committee agreed to 'wink at the existence of an illegal state of things for the modest term of six months'.

The second owner of interest, who belatedly also became a vestryman, was Harry Edward Busby, a wire worker from Birmingham, born in 1835. He moved into No.17 Wellington Square around 1870 and started to accumulate leases for houses in Wellington Square and Derry Street. By the mid-1880s he had eight houses and was agent for a few more.[23] Busby stayed in Wellington Square until the turn of the century but was not as successful as Gordon; he may not have had the latter's aspirations or ruthlessness. As a witness at several inquests he gives the impression of having a degree of empathy with his tenants. In 1897, for instance, Thomas O'Callhan died aged 59 at No.8 Derry Street. He had been an actor with the stage name of T C Harris; Busby described to the court how he was a 'noteworthy actor in his time' and how 'Sir Henry Irving saw that he did not want'.[24]

During the walking inspection in 1885 by the correspondent of *The Standard* and the sanitary inspector, there was an exchange with one of the house owners in Gray's Inn Road: 'There's one of 'em', he says. 'One what?' 'Why, landlord having his boots cleaned.' The correspondent adds 'The landlord does not look by any means pleased at being accosted....As we walk away I am told that the man is worth a great deal of money, yet it has always been the greatest worry possible to get him to do anything for his tenants.'[25] As it was a Sunday morning, this may have been Busby, but he can't have been worth 'a great deal of money'.

Busby was a resident landlord, and there were others in Cat's Meat Square over the years. Much of his property was previously leased by Cornelius McAuliffe, a Cork dairyman, who continued to occupy only one floor of No.13 and then of No.9 Derry Street in the 1860s.[26] Charles O'Brien leased a couple of houses at about the same time and his son John did so later. There are similar examples at the low end of the ownership structure, none of whom could be described as wealthy but who had the opportunity to sublet their way into a better standard of living. The number of Irish landlords, of which there were quite a few after 1840, no doubt also helped to maintain the 'Irish Colony' image.

Harry Busby became a member of the St Pancras Vestry in June 1884, possibly as the result of pressure from Gordon, who by then needed more allies as the press onslaught against the house farmers intensified. It was to be a short-lived membership. In April 1885, Gordon, Busby, fellow Ward 8 vestryman John Samuels and one other resigned,[27] ostensibly because of the 'qualification scandal' which swept London at the time. As a result of a legal ruling, vestrymen not holding property rated at £40 or more were deemed unqualified. This applied to many others on the St Pancras vestry, so it is strange, but significant, that these resignations took place just before the Royal Commission report was published. Gordon and the others were probably pressured into resigning by fellow vestrymen wishing to deflect criticism from themselves – they would have known from a draft of the report in February that St Pancras would be seen in an unflattering light.

John Samuels was a member of the Sanitary Committee, and seems to have been a significant ally of the property owners. A master watchmaker, he had lived in the district for many years and had a shop at No.1 Harrison Street in 1851; Jane Payne, wife of the original builder of Prospect Terrace, lived above.[28] Clearly, there was a network of small businessman, builders and shopkeepers looking after each others' interests. Payne's daughter Louisa Graham still recorded 'income from house property' as her occupation in 1871.[29] The Payne family evidently kept control of many of the original head leases on the Harrison Estate and the associated income for the rest of the century.

Other St Pancras vestrymen could be found as owners of insanitary property in Ward 8. During a debate in Parliament in March 1884, Sir Charles Dilke said that in 'St. Pancras some property, which had been repeatedly reported upon by the medical officer and condemned by the surveyor as buildings which ought to be demolished, belonged to a Vestryman whose father was, and whose grandfather had been on the Vestry.'[30] The property was Melina Place, off Cromer Street, and the landlords were the Eldridge family, small builders originally from Paddington. Thomas Eldridge was a significant local figure in the 1850s and 60s, often representing the vestry at London-wide meetings. He was also the owner in mid-century of Cooper's Buildings, again one of the worst Cromer Street courts.[31] Although Eldridge had almost certainly engineered the dismissal of two sanitary inspectors, he denied in January 1867 that it was the holders of small property in the vestry who had 'opposed the continuance of the late sanitary inspectors'.[32]

Another house farming family on the vestry was that of the Yollands, who were also in the building industry. Stephen Yolland was on the vestry for Ward 8 in the 1880s where his father Thomas had also been a vestryman. The Yollands held a large portfolio of houses around Cromer Street and elsewhere.[33] How many hard-core bad property owners were on the vestry is difficult to say; probably not more than 20 (out of 120), including their active supporters. However, a frustrated member of the Sanitary Committee revealed their tactics in the 1860s when he said that when the committee sought the sanction of the full vestry 'they were swamped by vestrymen who never attended, except upon such an occasion.'[34] The hard core could call upon the support of enough of the remaining vestry members when required.

Keeping down the rates was always a principal concern of vestrymen across London, but St Pancras was later to have a very good record in introducing public baths and was in the vanguard of installing electric lighting in its streets. Spending the ratepayers' money would not therefore have been an insurmountable issue if the will had been there. But the influence of the house farmers on the vestry ensured inaction on housing matters. They had a pecuniary interest in blocking reform. There were plenty of smaller vestries with equally dismal records in sanitary matters, but of the six large London vestries St Pancras probably had the poorest record.

Of the Prospect Terrace vestrymen, George Gordon died on 28 December 1905, a few months before most of his remaining property was demolished. He left £5,896, a not inconsiderable sum and much of it generated from rents extracted from some of the poorest people in London.[35] Busby had moved to No.31 Sidmouth Street in 1896 and later settled in Holloway. He died in December 1920, leaving the more modest sum of £1,153.[36]

Notes, chapter 7

RCHWC refers to the First Report (7 May 1885) of Her Majesty's Commission for Inquiring into the Housing of the Working Classes. Page numbers refer to pages in the Report itself, 'para' to a paragraph in the Minutes of Evidence appended to the Report. The third Volume contained the Index.

1 Hansard, 1 May 1889, Vol 335, debate on the Leasehold Enfranchisement Bill.

2 Evidence of John Bates, RCHWC, paras 4138, 4140.

3 RCHWC, Vol III Indexes, p 79.

4 RCHWC, para 4139.

5 *The Freeman's Journal*, 11 September 1875.

6 SPV Rate Books, 1872 (CLSAC).

7 SPV Rate Books, 1882 (CLSAC).

8 Evidence of Octavia Hill, RCHWC, para 8975.

9 SPV minute book, 30 March 1875, transcribed by John Richardson (CLSAC).

10 SPV Sanitary Committee minutes, 15 April 1885 (CLSAC).

11 *The Times*, 29 March 1844. Ground rents amounted to £1,795 from 300 properties.

12 1851 and 1861 England censuses, National Archives (Ancestry.co.uk).

13 *The Standard*, 23 September 1863.

14 Court for Divorce and Matrimonial Causes, 1858-1866 Series, G101, National Archives, Appellant: Catherine Garbit. Granted June 1864.

15 Church of the Holy Trinity, Gray's Inn Road, Marriage Register, 15 March 1865 (Ancestry.co.uk).

16 1871 England Census, National Archives (Ancestry.co.uk).

17 MDR/1862/5/715, 25 March 1862 (LMA).

18 SPV Rate Books, 1866 (CLSAC).

19 SPV minute book, 2 June 1869, transcribed by John Richardson (CLSAC).

20 *Daily News*, 20 December 1876.

21 1891 England Census, National Archives (Ancestry.co.uk). Gordon was registered at No.7 Prospect Terrace from 1884 to preserve voting and vestry rights.

22 *St Pancras Guardian*, 2 January 1885.

23 SPV Rate Books, 1880-5 (CLSAC).

24 *Illustrated Police News*, 16 January 1897.

25 *The Standard*, 22 September 1885.

26 SPV Rate Books and Census data.

27 *St Pancras Gazette*, 25 April 1885.

28 1851 England Census, National Archives (Ancestry.co.uk).

29 1871 England Census, National Archives (Ancestry.co.uk).

30 Hansard, 4 March 1884, Vol 285, Debate on Dwellings in Crowded Districts.

31 SPV Rate Books, 1850-1869 (CLSAC).

32 *The Times*, 11 January 1867.

33 SPV Rate Books 1850-1885 and SPV minutes.

34 *The Times*, 11 January 1867.

35 National Probate Calendar (Index of Wills and Administrations), 1861-1941 (Ancestry.co.uk).

36 Ibid.

8 The housing crisis comes to a head: the Royal Commission

(Notes for this chapter on p 49)

In 1883 the Rev Andrew Mearns published a short book entitled *The Bitter Cry of Outcast London.*[1] Victorian hyperbole at its best, it caused a sensation and is generally credited with spawning the Royal Commission on the Housing of the Working Classes, which was set up the following year. The crisis in housing in London had been growing for decades, but Mearn's pamphlet spurred the debate as nothing had before. Key figures who would form part of the Royal Commission such as Lords Shaftesbury and Carrington, former Home Secretary Richard Cross and Sir Charles Dilke [14] had long been interested in the London housing issue and Dilke in particular had started visiting some of the worst areas, including south St Pancras. However, a prominent figure was needed to feature in the process, and there was none better than the Prince of Wales, who agreed to be a member.

In the run-up to the Commission's work, Carrington suggested to the Prince that he should undertake a discreet visit to selected insanitary areas, and Holborn

and St Pancras were chosen as both representative and easily accessible. On 18 February 1884 the Prince, Carrington and Dr Buchanan (the government's Chief Medical Officer) set off disguised as sanitary workers (the Prince wearing a 'slouch hat' and 'clothes of a very seedy sort')[2], following a route up Gray's Inn Road. They first visited Dove Court[3] in the group of dismal alleys and streets between Leather Lane and Gray's Inn Road. Which area in St Pancras they visited is not known: it could have been Cat's

[14] Sir Charles Wentworth Dilke, 2nd Bt. (1843-1911), chairman of the Royal Commission on the Housing of the Working Classes. Portrait by G F Watts, 1873. A leading Liberal politician of the day, his political career was ruined by a sex scandal a year after the Commission's report was published.

Meat Square but might equally well have been one of the small courts off Cromer Street or Poplar Place which the vestry had recently resolved to demolish. Carrington later recounted how the landlord of one house (unaware of who he was speaking to) guided them into a filthy room where a mother and her semi-naked children lived in complete squalor. "What on earth are we to do with people of that sort?" asked the landlord. The Prince is alleged to have been so shocked he was about to toss a handful of sovereigns at the woman but was persuaded that the inhabitants of the court would tear them apart.[4]

Four days later, the Prince made a rare speech[5] in the House of Lords: 'Only a few days ago I visited two of the poorest courts and districts in St Pancras and in Holborn, where I can assure your Lordships that the condition of the poor, or rather of their dwellings, was perfectly disgraceful.' *Reynold's News* was not impressed, saying 'it appears he took a stroll through some of the lanes, alleys and courts of St Pancras'. The Prince was merely an 'ornamental figure-head' according to the newspaper.[6]

The Royal Commission met sporadically from March 1884 for nearly a year to consider housing conditions in England and Wales, with Sir Charles Dilke as chairman. Later reports dealt with Scotland and Ireland. HRH the Prince of Wales attended the first four sessions but soon prioritised other interests and rarely turned up. A part of London was chosen for 'minute investigation' by the Commission, the arc just north of the centre. This was because, Dilke was to say, 'the central parts of London, including parts of St Luke's, nearly the whole of Clerkenwell, the southern part of St Pancras, and the eastern part of Holborn, were by very far the worst parts of London, both as regards the structural condition of the houses, and also as regards overcrowding'.[7] Clerkenwell was singled out for the most opprobrium, it being well known for both its lack of action and the large number of vestrymen owning bad property. Dilke provided evidence that 14 vestrymen owned slum property in the parish.

St Pancras was also one of the main targets and much hinged on extensive evidence from Dr Shirley F Murphy, who had been the vestry Medical Officer of Health for the previous six years. Dr Murphy was himself of Irish heritage, the son of George Murphy, a St Pancras pianoforte manufacturer. He had developed an interest in public health as one of the first resident surgeons at the Homerton Fever Hospital. The Commission's report, published on 7 May 1885, particularly praised the 'excellent medical officer' of St Pancras and said that in Wellington Square, 'which was stated in evidence [by Murphy] to belong to a member of the St Pancras Vestry', the death rate in 1882 was '53.7 per thousand, and in Derry Street 44.4 per thousand'.[8] These were very high mortality rates; the London average was around 20 at this time and in the Old Nichol area of Bethnal Green, one of the capital's most infamous slums, death rates averaged 40 in the 1880s.

Murphy gave evidence over two days in March 1884, with HRH attending the second session. Overcrowding was still increasing, he said, most recently because of the 'demolition of houses by the Midland Railway Company. About 500 houses in Somers Town have been removed'. Despite the relevant Act obliging the Company to offer alternative accommodation, he confirmed that none had been provided and that to a large extent the displaced population had gone into the southern portion of the parish. Murphy said there was space for about 2,000 persons in 'model lodgings' in St Pancras but that the rents were distinctly too high for the poor. Conversely, there were 'about 5,500 tenement houses in which the landlord is not resident. Then there are about 10,000 houses which are let in lodgings, but where the landlord resides on the premises'.[9] There were 24,700 houses in total in St Pancras, meaning the parish had one of the highest percentage of tenement houses in London – over 60%.

However, the tenements could not be inspected at night (when overcrowding was at its highest level) unless the houses were registered as lodging houses under the 1866 Sanitary Act. Dilke asked Murphy whether the tenement provisions had been adopted and he replied 'We have not adopted them in St Pancras' although he had recommended this 'several times'.

"You have frequently recommended the vestry to put the tenements provisions in force and make byelaws? – Yes." "But they have never done so? – They have never done so."[10]

Prevarication by the vestry under the Torrens' Act (p 28) was also laid bare. Murphy confirmed that the vestry had 'determined to allow the houses to be repaired' in Melina Place, which he confirmed was owned by a vestryman, despite his recommendation to demolish. He also criticised the small number of sanitary inspectors in the parish.[11]

But he also outlined some recent improvement, saying that the vestry had 'done a great deal lately'. Murphy had had success in getting demolition orders on the worst houses in Cooper's Buildings, Catel Place (both in Cromer Street) and Poplar Place agreed by the vestry. Dilke asked '...a great stir has been made and you consequently feel yourself supported by public opinion?' Murphy agreed. Sanitary Committee members were of late at pains to emphasise how they were unaware of the worst conditions and were 'horrified at what they had seen'.[12]

Asked what would be his priorities for immediate action by the vestry, Dr Murphy replied that Melina Place and the other bad Cromer Street courts should be pulled down and that Derry Street and Prospect Terrace would 'have to be demolished shortly'. He had earlier outlined the structural differences in the Prospect Terrace area: 'Some of the houses in Wellington Square are not specially unsanitary with regard to their construction, they are old houses and have been roughly handled by the people living in them; but some of the houses in Derry Street are back-to-back houses. The houses in Prospect Terrace have no backs; they abut on the houses in Derry Street ... I am quite prepared to say that back-to-back houses, such as those in Derry

Street and Prospect Terrace, are not what may be called healthy habitations'.[13]

The back-to-back house was complete anathema to sanitary reformers of the time. For the Victorians, nothing better could mitigate against the threat of disease than good through-ventilation, plainly impossible where only one elevation had windows. For the deprived occupants, however, they did have the advantage that the houses were easier to keep warm in the depths of winter (generally more severe than those of today), and the potent mix of body odours, smoke and herrings was probably considered a small price to pay.

Evidence was also taken from Inspector John Bates of the Metropolitan Police. He explained that in Prospect Terrace 'there are 16 seven-roomed houses, they are let at 17s 6d a week, and are again sub-let. Sometimes families pay 4s 6d for one room and 5s 6d for two .... I went into one house, No.10, and I spoke to a woman who was living in the parlour on the left-hand side. She looked very ill. She and her husband and four children were occupying this room. One little boy was lying on the floor, and the woman told me that they had not seen meat since Christmas time .... She told me that the landlord refused to take her money because she was a halfpenny short in the rent. She had 4s 5d and a halfpenny wherewith to pay 4s 6d, and the landlord, or rather his agent, positively refused to take her money, and told her she had better put it in a flower pot until it grew; and she sold her bedstead to raise the money for the rent'.[14]

A weekly rent of 17s 6d was a typical price that Gordon and his fellow landlords paid to lease houses from either middlemen or head lessees such as the Paynes and their successors. Upwards of 10s a week profit could be made from each house, producing a very good income if enough houses were held. The Commission heard examples of house farmers making £80 a year profit from a single house, for rents had more than doubled in less than 20 years. The houses were in such poor condition by the 1880s, however, that even if all the profit had been spent on renovations, it would not be enough to bring them up to a reasonable standard. In fact the landlords spent virtually nothing and the freeholders did little to enforce the repairing obligations of the leases. No.10 Prospect Terrace was not one of Gordon's houses but he may well have been the agent.

Richard Cobden, a London School Board visitor for south St Pancras, was also questioned. He confirmed the recent increase in overcrowding in the district, saying 'a great number of them have come from where the Midland Railway have pulled property down. They were people that I knew well'. He was of the view that displaced people rarely went out of the parish but 'keep moving from one place to another'. He described another family in No.10 Prospect Terrace, this time with eight in the one room and at No.3 Derry Street (one of Gordon's properties) a family of nine people occupied the first-floor front room with one bed, paying 4s a week. Cobden thought that many of the 'respectable' working class were being driven into these areas by the economic depression and high rents.[15] This reflected a wider realisation in the mid-1880s that the occupiers of insanitary areas were not merely composed of the so-called residuum – the workless, costermongers and such like – but included a much broader spectrum of the working class.

The Royal Commission report in 1885 ([15], p 48) was not only a milestone in housing policy but marked a significant change from the moralising and demonization of the poor to an acceptance that greater intervention by the state was necessary. Low wages, casualisation and the need to live close to opportunities for work were all recognised as contributing to the housing crisis in central London; but proposals for resolution of the problem were limited. More cheap workman's trains was one suggestion, and there was some recognition that local authorities should be allowed greater freedom to build housing themselves – although subsidisation from the rates was still not acceptable. The failure of the London vestries to use powers available to them was stressed and 'it seemed that in some cases the authority had almost forgotten that they had powers'.[8]

Referring to St Pancras, the report said that: "...it has been sufficiently backward to decline to follow the medical officer's recommendation to adopt the tenement provisions of the Sanitary Act. Nevertheless by continual vigilance and activity he thoroughly investigated the condition of the district, and he put himself in a position to use all the power that is placed in his hands. Your Majesty's Commissioners much regret to notice that during the revision of their report the medical officer in question found himself compelled to resign on account of his relations with his vestry".[16]

Dr Murphy had resigned in March 1885, citing in his letter 'the most exceptional and unscrupulous means' to discredit him and 'an almost hopeless struggle against interests opposed to sanitary reform'.[17] The vestry had set up a special committee to investigate the sanitary department following allegations that Murphy had suppressed information that should have been reported to the vestry – subsequently disproved. There can be no doubt that some members of the vestry were determined to emasculate Murphy's work in St Pancras, if not oust him altogether. Following the reading of Dr Murphy's letter at the next vestry meeting, vestryman James Watkins was reported as saying: 'After that insulting letter I shall move without further comment that the resignation be accepted', and vestryman Fox added 'I have very great pleasure in seconding that. He has just saved his bacon'.[18]

Murphy had clearly been emboldened by the Royal Commission's reaction to his evidence. He had the backing of some of the most powerful politicians in the land, not to mention the implicit support of the Prince of Wales. His activity in condemning bad property did not slacken. In January he had served improvement notices on Cat's Meat Square, and on the day he submitted his resignation in

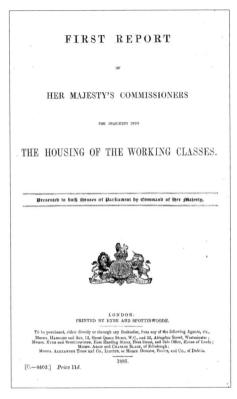

FIRST REPORT

OF

HER MAJESTY'S COMMISSIONERS

FOR INQUIRING INTO

THE HOUSING OF THE WORKING CLASSES.

Presented to both Houses of Parliament by Command of Her Majesty.

LONDON:
PRINTED BY EYRE AND SPOTTISWOODE.

To be purchased, either directly or through any Bookseller, from any of the following Agents, viz.,
Messrs. HANSARD and SON, 13, Great Queen Street, W.C., and 32, Abingdon Street, Westminster;
Messrs. EYRE and SPOTTISWOODE, East Harding Street, Fleet Street, and Sale Office, House of Lords;
Messrs. ADAM and CHARLES BLACK, of Edinburgh;
Messrs. ALEXANDER THOM and Co., LIMITED, or Messrs. HODGES, FIGGIS, and Co., of Dublin.

1885.

[C.—4402.] Price 11d.

March, a whole raft of properties (mainly around Cromer Street) was recommended as unfit for habitation in the Medical Officer of Health report to the Sanitary Committee. Vestryman Cook was reported as denouncing the 'wholesale condemnation' of houses and 'was not sorry to hear that afternoon that he had resigned his appointment'.[18] Dr Murphy was defended by others, notably Nathan Robinson, the chair of the Sanitary Committee for some years, whom Murphy had praised in his evidence to the Commission. Robinson attacked the owners of 'rotten unsanitary old property' and said Murphy had been a 'most valuable and trustworthy officer'.[18]

The St Pancras Guardian said[19] the resignation was 'another nail driven into the coffin of government by vestrydom' and that Murphy 'had offended, on more than one occasion, the delicate susceptibilities of the house-farming fraternity, and that sooner or later he would have to pay the consequences of his own temerity'. It added that 'the interests opposed to sanitary reform may rejoice at the Doctor's departure, the poor may come to regret it'. The Pall Mall Gazette remarked[20] that it was a 'public loss' and that no other medical officer had been more 'energetic or successful'. Dilke immediately gave Murphy a position in the Local Government Board at twice the salary and in May the vestry appointed Dr John Frederick Sykes as its new medical officer.

This show of strength by the house farmers and their supporters in securing Murphy's resignation was ultimately undermined by the publication of the Royal Commission report, preceded by George Gordon's resignation. In February 1886 Murphy's final annual report was presented to the Sanitary Committee in his absence and Nathan Robinson (possibly taking advantage of the slight shift in power) proposed that 'the best thanks of the vestry be engrossed on vellum and, with the corporate seal of the vestry attached, be presented to Dr Murphy'. 'Hear, hear' went around the room.[21] St Pancras Vestry had not heard the last of Dr Shirley Murphy, however [16], and Cat's Meat Square still had 20 years of life left.

[16] Sir Shirley Foster Murphy, KBE, FRCS (1843-1923), 1909. He was Medical Officer of St Pancras from 1878 until 1885 and the first Chief Medical Officer of the LCC from 1889 until 1914. He was knighted in 1904 for services to public health.

12 Ibid, paras 1643-1644.

13 Ibid, paras 1690-1693.

14 Evidence of Inspector John Bates, RCHWC paras 4138-4140.

15 Evidence of Richard Cobden, RCHWC paras 4689-4810.

16 First Report of Her Majesty's Commissioners for Inquiring into the Housing of the Working Classes, 7 May 1885, p 34.

17 Reproduced in the St Pancras Guardian, 7 March 1885. The resignation was timed to coincide with the publication of the RCHWC report and must have been agreed with Dilke, who included the reference to resignation in the report before Murphy issued his letter.

18 St Pancras Gazette, 5 March 1885. James Watkins was a stalwart of the vestry and the Board of Guardians.

19 St Pancras Guardian, 7 March 1885.

20 Pall Mall Gazette, 26 March 1885.

21 The Daily News, 4 February 1886.

Notes, chapter 8

1 Mearns, Andrew, The Bitter Cry of Outcast London, 1883.

2 St Aubyn, Giles, Edward VII, Prince and King, 1979, p 253 and The Ipswich Journal, 23 February 1884.

3 RCHWC, para 1554.

4 Carrington recounted the visit to the first-class passengers of the ship The Scot in 1891, reported in the North Ortago Times, 19 October 1891.

5 Hansard, 22 February 1884, Vol 284, Debate on Housing of the Working Classes.

6 Reynold's Newspaper, 24 February 1884.

7 RCHWC para 17582.

8 First Report of Her Majesty's RCHWC, 7 May 1885, p 14.

9 Evidence of Dr S F Murphy, RCHWC paras 1576-1596.

10 Ibid, paras 1603-1608.

11 Ibid, paras 1622-1625.

9 The School Board and the LCC intervene, 1885-1900

(Notes for this chapter on p 63)

The second half of the 1880s saw some progress in combating the insanitary areas in Ward 8 of St Pancras, spurred on by the furore surrounding the Royal Commission report. Much of the Cromer Street area was pulled down at the end of the decade, to be replaced by Whidborne House and other blocks of the East End Dwellings Company development. Poplar Place was finally cleared in December 1885 amid 'extraordinary and distressing scenes'.[1] Some 240 people lived in tiny houses in the inter-connecting Poplar and Compton Places. The landlord had disappeared owing £120 in fines, having repeatedly failed to comply with improvement orders. There was no water supply and much of the woodwork, including staircases, had been used for fuel. Vestry officials and workmen started clearing the houses, 'the things from the upper floors being moved by the simple expedient of throwing them from the windows'. Some refused to go, having nowhere to move to, and the police were called to assist. 'In one case a poor old woman of about 60, partly paralysed, was found in a room without furniture, sleeping on a heap of waste paper and covered with a couple of old rags. She was sent to the workhouse in a cab'.

The Poplar Place evictions vividly illustrated once again the lack of affordable housing. Conditions here had degenerated to an appalling level and could not be ignored, but the end result would be still more overcrowding as the residents found their way to other poor areas such as Prospect Terrace. Charles Booth published the first edition of his poverty maps of London in 1889-90 and these show all the Ward 8 insanitary areas still intact, coloured dark blue and black, the very poor, destitute and semi-criminal categories [17].

In Cat's Meat Square, change of a different order was in the air. The School Board for London was busy erecting new school buildings across the capital following the 1870 Education Act. Preferred sites were often occupied by insanitary houses – two birds could be killed with one stone. Wellington Square was proposed for a 1200-place school by 1884, catering for the increased population in the area. But the school would displace some 300 people and this did not go unchallenged. In a memorandum to the School Board in March 1886, the vicars of St Peter's Regent Square and St Jude's Gray's Inn Road, together with the President of the Home and Colonial Training College in Gray's Inn Road, called for the proposed school to be abandoned as a 'wasteful and unnecessary expenditure of the ratepayers' money'.[2] They said it would be 'undesirable to destroy so many homes of the poor in the already over-populated parish of St Peter' where in the ten years to 1881 the population had increased by 'nearly 4000, without the additional erection of a single house'.

It was clear, however, that the primary objection was the impact additional school places might have on the Home and Colonial training college and St Jude's

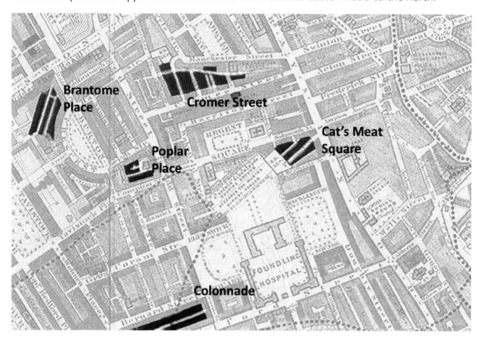

[17] Ward 8 of St Pancras in the mid-1880s. Based on the 1889 edition of Charles Booth's poverty maps of London. Black areas correspond to Booth's dark blue and black. Parish boundary marked by dotted line; ward 8 was bounded by Tavistock Square and Upper Woburn Place to the west and Euston Road to the north.

school, both Anglican, and said to be not up to capacity. It was claimed the Home and Colonial had already lost 60 pupils because the fees were lower in nearby Board schools. The School Board was chaired by the Rev Joseph Diggle, renowned for his attempts to reduce expenditure. The Progressive (Liberal) wing of the Board adopted the term "Diggleism" to describe the alleged deliberate underfunding of secular education in order to favour Anglican schools. Diggle favoured shelving the proposed school and after much internal discussion, and in a classic fudge, it was resolved in October 1886 to replace the proposal for a 1200-place school with one for 800 places which could be enlarged if necessary.[3]

The School Board had placed compulsory purchase notices in the press in November 1884 for fourteen houses in Wellington Square and a further five in Prospect Terrace, totalling about 12,000 sq ft.[4] George Gordon's delaying tactics over improvement orders on his houses (p 39) took advantage of the protracted compensation negotiations with the School Board. Wrangling over the size of the school dragged on for years, adding uncertainty as to the future of Cat's Meat Square. The freehold interests of the school site were bought from the Harrison Estate for £5,100 in 1886[5] and the leasehold interests (including 'James Payne or those claiming under him', the Carr family and Gordon and Busby) over subsequent years.[6] Harry Busby was paid £54 compensation in 1890, as the new school was 'injuriously affecting light and air' to his remaining houses in Wellington Square, which were actually some 25 ft away.[7]

[18] Architect's drawing of Prospect Terrace School,
north-east elevation facing Derry Street.
The tower is shown as it was eventually built.

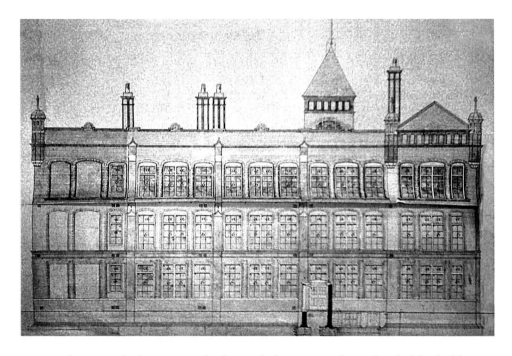

A change in the law in 1882 had provided a way out for embattled freeholders by removing the obligation to inherit. Thomas Harrison's son Daniel died in 1873 and the latter's first son, Daniel Alfred, drowned at sea in July 1885. His son, Alfred Henry Harrison, opted to pursue a career as a polar explorer and disposed of much of the family property after overturning the terms of Thomas Harrison's will. The freehold interests of the Harrison Estate, in whole or in parts, were put on the market in 1885, 1887 and 1888, when they were claimed to be in an 'unsurpassable position for letting'.[8] All the original head leases were to fall in during 1901 and there was much trading in the fag ends of the leases in the final 15 years. An Arthur Rickarby took a number of houses in Prospect Terrace and offered them for (compensated) demolition. Harrison Estates Ltd continued well into the 20th century but by 1902 the number of houses and shops it owned had decreased to 133, well under half the original number.[9]

The new school was designed in the classic School Board Queen Anne style [18] and was the usual three storeys high with a playground at roof level as the site was constricted. The architect's original drawings suggest that there was cost-cutting at the design stage: the amount of ornament on the top floor was reduced, and the central tower, which was originally intended to match St Peter's Regent Square in prominence, was considerably reduced in height. Most interestingly, the design[10] included small Islamic-inspired capped turrets at the corners, which survived the cost reductions.

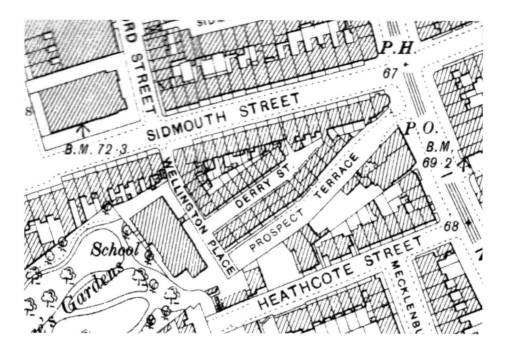

The school when built obliterated the whole of Wellington Square except for its east side, which was incorporated into Wellington Place [19]. It was ready in August 1890 and at the formal opening in October the Rev Diggle observed that the school was 'one of the best that had been erected' and that the 'scholars would in and after life benefit by the tuition they would receive'.[11] A year later the *Pall Mall Gazette* was attacking 'School Board penny wisdom', as it had now been resolved to enlarge it to the originally mooted 1200 places.[12] In fact, the enlargement never took place. The 1891 census recorded 590 people in Cat's Meat Square, which by extrapolation means that just under 300 people were displaced by the school if the density per room of remaining houses is used for those that were lost.[13] There is no indication of any eviction scenes like those at Poplar Place a few years earlier, but given the unrelenting pace of demolitions in the late 1880s and 90s across north central London, finding alternative housing must have been very difficult.

Prospect Terrace School prospered; it provided infant and junior classes for the local population. Some signs of conflict between the ethos of the School Board and the locals of Cat's Meat Square are evident – by 1898 the management of the Gray's Inn Road Group of Board Schools were writing to the vestry complaining of the 'low and rough approaches to the Prospect Terrace School' and that as a result there are 'cases of children who are kept away from school because they would have to pass through these places'.[14] Young women were deterred from attending the Evening Continuation School for the same reason. An article in *Lloyd's Weekly* in

November 1902, referring to the Prospect Terrace School [20], quipped[15] that it was built on a site that 'once was that notorious preparatory school for Newgate known as Catsmeat square'.

Life in Cat's Meat Square continued much as before the demolitions. The census of 1891 showed population density at roughly the same levels as 1881. It continued to show a downward trend of Irish-born heads of households, now just 8.5%. Another 9.5% were born outside the county of London. Of those born in London, 26% had been born in St Pancras, followed by Clerkenwell, and smaller numbers from Holborn, St Giles and Strand district. This supports the observations of commentators of the times – the poor in the centre of London were being squeezed into fewer and smaller areas and had not moved further out. But there was now a marked decline of new incomers into central London; the suburbs were increasingly drawing the new arrivals and industry was relocating there too.

The common allegation in the press that Prospect Terrace was principally a haven for costermongers and hawkers (Irish or otherwise) is supported to some extent by this census. Fifteen heads of households fell into this category (costers, hawkers, general dealers, shoeblacks etc), but the wives and offspring of others were also involved in the trade. This was an increase on previous years, though by no means a majority, and reflects the loss of housing nearer the central markets. A verbal exchange[16] at a coroner's inquest in January 1893 demonstrated the precariousness of life in Cat's Meat Square: the son of Mary Ann Donnelly of No.9 Derry Street, on being told that no doctor from the Royal Free Hospital could attend to his seriously

[21] Brantome Place from the north east, 1897.
It contained 32 houses which in 1884 housed
98 families with over 230 children.
The left turning led to North Crescent Mews.

ill mother at home, wheeled her across Gray's Inn Road on his barrow. On arrival at the hospital she was pronounced dead. The coroner remarked that 'she must have been dying when you removed her', to which the son replied: 'That was why I took her to the hospital'. The coroner, clearly alarmed that bodies were being wheeled about on barrows, thought that 'there were proper conveyances – ambulances – for the removal of the sick' but was informed by the resident medical officer that the hospital did not have one.

Towards the end of the decade, some on the radical wing of the vestry such as Henry Lazarus began independent inspections of insanitary property, followed up by a private summons of the landlord, thereby bypassing the vestry. Lazarus had some success in promoting the cause of sanitary reform – in 1889 he had vigorously opposed the proposed membership on the Sanitary Committee of vestryman Page, who he alleged was the owner of bad property in Drummond Street. Page lost the vote. Lazarus' campaign prompted *Reynold's Newspaper* to declare[17] that 'the vestry of St Pancras are probably dead to shame' and urged them to 'abandon the friendship of the house farmer and take some action against insanitary dwellings'. The *British Medical Journal* said the vestry 'is to be congratulated in having amongst its numbers an earnest sanitary reformer in Mr Lazarus'.[18] Lazarus unsuccessfully stood for election to the LCC as an independent in 1892.

The London County Council had been formed in 1889 and some LCC members employed the same tactics as Lazarus. Alfred Davies 'deserves public thanks' according to *Reynold's Newspaper*, which again attacked 'that shameful body the St Pancras vestry'.[19] The advent of the LCC fundamentally changed the balance of power in London, and the widely discredited vestrydom was now in its last decade. Dr Shirley Murphy became the LCC's first Chief Medical Officer, and although there is no evidence he bore a grudge against St Pancras, he must have been pleased to see the cause of sanitary reform make some progress in the parish. Failures by vestries across London to use legislation open to them now felt the pressure applied by the LCC, which also enacted its own housing schemes; the large and

[22] North Crescent Mews from the south west (Dixon photograph, 1897) was originally built to service Burton Crescent, out of view to the right. Taller houses to the left are those of Brantome Place.

vocal vestries such as St Pancras were the main targets.

By the start of the 1890s the vestry at last recognised that three areas in south St Pancras urgently needed housing schemes. The Prospect Terrace area, Brantome Place and Churchway were the most pressing; the main problem was to find the necessary funding. Brantome Place ([21], p 55) previously known as Drapers Place, lay at the back of Burton Crescent (now Cartwright Gardens), and the equally grim North Crescent Mews [22] ran alongside it. The site of both is today occupied by Flaxman Terrace and its block of dwellings. During the 1880s overcrowding had increased and despite improvement schemes run by one of Octavia Hill's associates, the area had degenerated into a squalid slum. Churchway, just north of Euston Road across from St Pancras church, was the worst of the Somers Town areas. It was a narrow path marking the boundary between the Somers and Southampton estates, flanked by dilapidated housing [23].

In December 1890, Dr Sykes had made representations on the part of St Pancras

[23] Entrance to Churchway from Euston Road. A new street was driven through leading to the LCC's Churchway flats of 1901. On the right is the former Elizabeth Garrett Anderson Hospital, opened as the New Hospital for Women in 1890.

vestry requesting the LCC to act on all three areas under part I of the Housing of the Working Classes Act 1890. The vestry hoped that the LCC would pay the full cost. The 1890 Act was the first to explicitly encourage London local authorities to build housing for rent, envisaging large schemes to be carried out by the LCC and smaller schemes by vestries under part II. The Council duly ruled in May 1891 that Dr Sykes' schemes should be carried out by the vestry.[20] The vestry took the view that the LCC's opinion was 'wholly unfavourable to the interests of St Pancras'[21] and petitioned the Home Secretary to arbitrate. An inquiry was set up and quickly adjourned, to resume in February 1893.

The LCC maintained that 'a parish like St Pancras, having a gross rateable value of £2,000,000, should not expect the metropolis generally to bear the whole cost of clearing away its defective dwellings'.[22] St Pancras had yet to plan a single dwelling, unlike a number of other vestries such as Shoreditch which now embraced the times and started building. The Home Secretary's decision, in June 1893, was that Cat's Meat Square and Brantome Place should be dealt with by the vestry, with the LCC contributing half the cost. The LCC were to reconstruct most of the Churchway area with the vestry undertaking a small part.[23]

The LCC had produced a plan for the 1891 Inquiry showing a possible solution for Prospect Terrace/Derry Street [24]. It estimated that 542 people would be displaced and housing for 200 provided on the site. It was not until January 1896, however, that the vestry finally resolved[24] to adopt almost the same scheme housing 200 people, drawn up by the LCC's surveyor Keith Young. The lack of progress over 5 years vividly illustrates the vestry's reluctance to spend on this and the other sites despite the obvious need: in December 1894 the Gray's Inn Lane sub-district had the highest death rate in St Pancras, at nearly 21 per 1,000 population.[25] Delays were about to get worse as the vestry and the LCC squabbled over the housing schemes.

The 1890 Act required a reasonable number of re-housed tenants, the Local Government Board having the final say if there was no agreement on what was 'reasonable'. The LCC wanted 800 new dwellings and insisted St Pancras find an additional site for new blocks. The vestry pointed out, not unreasonably, that Ward 8 was 'completely built upon'; the LGB responded[26] that the additional site could be outside Ward 8.

In a report to the vestry Dr Sykes estimated[27] that 1,300 people would be ousted from Prospect Terrace and Brantome Place, and the proposed developments would house only a third of this number. He pointed out that 'there are on the Prospect Terrace area more than three times and very nearly four times as many people as ought to be there' and that re-housing schemes cannot 'be expected to provide for more than one half of the population displaced and in most cases…for more than one third'. Sykes, while appearing to back the vestry view, was treading a fine line.

[24] The LCC's 1891 proposal for redeveloping Cat's Meat Square:
to build a single four-storey block (the dark area superimposed
on the existing houses) accommodating 200 people.

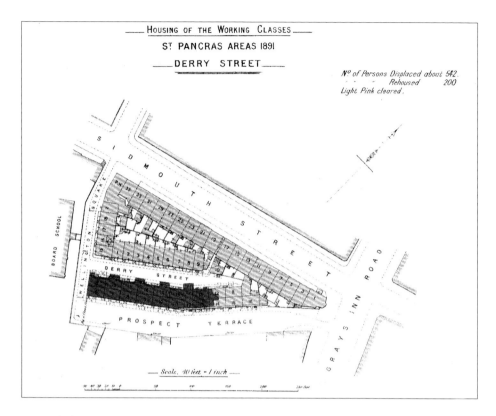

He said that the poor 'have been displaced from other districts by the conversion of
dwelling houses into workplaces...and those who trade in them have not been called
upon to provide housing for those they have displaced. That duty is now cast upon
your authority'.

The vestry stuck to its position that only a third of the displaced would be re-
housed and that any more 'would be a heavy burden on the ratepayers'. In reality,
though, nobody believed that the new dwellings would be occupied by any but a
handful of those in the insanitary areas, as the rents were too high. The debate was
more about the total housing stock. Some thought that 'levelling up' would ensure
that the poor would move into the better tenements vacated by those who could afford
the new blocks, so there would be a gradual improvement in conditions for all.

The vestry finally capitulated in July 1898 and accepted that it would have to
acquire land for a third re-housing scheme. After nearly another year, a site was at
last chosen on the corner of Great College Street and St Pancras Way, then in use as
a stoneyard but previously earmarked for municipal offices. This was eventually to
become Goldington Buildings, the first St Pancras municipal housing development.
The LGB, LCC and vestry continued to argue over the detail right up to the end of
vestrydom but although this dispute now appeared to be moving to resolution, the

frustration with delays in St Pancras was already provoking another issue.

Dr Sykes had long been unhappy with the number of sanitary inspectors employed by the parish, a view inherited from Dr Murphy, who had raised it in evidence to the Royal Commission in 1884, and from Drs Hillier and Stevenson before him. Under pressure from Sykes, the vestry Health Committee recommended in March 1898 two additional inspectors, which the full vestry meeting turned down.[28] The LCC reacted by instructing Dr William Hamer, one of Murphy's assistant medical officers, to investigate the sanitary condition of St Pancras. The result was to be another blow to St Pancras' image in the field of housing and sanitary reform.

The LCC sent Hamer's report to the vestry in October 1898. Instead of two, it recommended seven additional sanitary inspectors, backed up by detailed and lengthy evidence.[29] Doubtless it was Dr Murphy who initiated the LCC investigation against his old employer and Sykes probably knew about the LCC's agenda and approved of it. Murphy may have wanted a final, decisive act against St Pancras before vestries were abolished across London, only a couple of years away. Murphy's introduction to Hamer's report notes that St Pancras finally introduced by-laws for the regulation of tenement houses in 1893 but that there were currently only 166 houses on the register, even though the report showed that 'St Pancras contains a larger number of persons living in tenements of one and two rooms than any other London sanitary district'.

Dr Hamer showed that the Gray's Inn Lane sub-district (essentially Ward 8) had a population density of 191 per acre, the highest in the parish; and, taking into account mortality rates, that Somers Town and Gray's Inn Lane were 'eminently unsatisfactory'. St Pancras as a whole had worse overcrowding than had Whitechapel and Mile End in 1894. The worst examples were in streets with groups of houses, all of which groups were in common ownership. This reference to house farmers unfortunately did not name the landlords, vestrymen or locations. Undoubtedly Prospect Terrace was one of them.

Around the same time, the LCC debated a report from the Housing Committee in which the socialist MP and LCC member John Burns said he had visited Prospect Terrace and the surrounding streets the previous day with a clergyman. 'There were growing up there at least a dozen Boundary Street areas. In some respects they were even worse, because in Boundary Street [the Old Nichol area of Bethnal Green] they had only to deal with criminals coupled with the very poor, but in the Prospect Terrace district a new element was growing up – men who were living on women, the lowest of the low'.[30] Burns was a keen supporter of the temperance movement and, despite his radical and trade union background, was not sympathetic to the "residuum". He may have been influenced by the unnamed clergyman during this visit, who was possibly the Rev Charles Ensor Walters, a campaigning Methodist preacher from the London Wesleyan Mission, later the chairman of the Public Health Committee in the new borough. Apart from this, there is no evidence that prostitution was a major problem in Cat's Meat Square. Parts of the Cromer Street area did have prostitutes, according to Booth, but the worst that could be said about Cat's Meat Square was the significant number of households headed by widowed women working as charwomen and laundresses, with working-age sons employed or not.

In response to Hamer's report, the vestry Health Committee proposed acceptance of the findings but the vestry as a whole refused to, and set up a special committee to defend itself, which reported in May the following year.[31] It tried to blame other vestries for enforcing sanitary laws and the LCC for not re-housing the displaced tenants, and claimed that the investigation had alleged 'serious imputations of neglect of duty' by the vestry and 'done much to injure the reputation of this Parish'. It noted that the press had picked up the story and "Insanitary St Pancras" had been the heading of many paragraphs. Indeed, the liberal *Daily News* ran a report[32] of a packed public meeting held in March 1899 at the Passmore Edwards Settlement in Tavistock Place to 'protest against the conduct of the vestry in refusing to carry out the recommendation of its own Health Committee to appoint additional sanitary inspectors'. Letters of support were read, including one from vestry member George Bernard Shaw, who sent apologies saying that 'after 18 years' residence in the parish his state of health would not permit his attendance'.

The Rev Walters moved a resolution calling on the vestry to implement the recommendations. The Rev John J Coxhead seconded it, and recounted a story of a baby being kept in a chest of drawers to protect it from the rats that overran the family's basement room. The meeting may have been set up by the Progressives (Liberals). The vestry was at this time dominated by the Moderates (Conservatives), and the fight over sanitary reform had as much to do with jockeying for the forthcoming borough council elections as the issue itself. The Rev Coxhead (of St John the Evangelist, Fitzroy Square and formerly a member of the School Board) was actually a Moderate; the issue often crossed party lines.

Churchwarden W H Matthews (in effect the chairman of the vestry) braved the crowd and opposed the resolution, and was reported as saying that the vestry were 'practically powerless' to prevent the evils, but were doing 'all in their power to alleviate them'. He believed they had enough inspectors and that 'any addition was quite unnecessary'. The resolution was adopted by a 'large majority'.

William H Matthews had been Hon Secretary of the South St Pancras Conservative Association for 25 years and ran a greengrocer's shop at 276 Gray's Inn Road. The Association had its office and club at 262 Gray's Inn Road, just by the entrance to

Cubitt's yard. Matthews' shop was diagonally opposite Prospect Terrace, on the corner with Ampton Street, and he must have known many of the people who lived there well. He was later to complain that the demolition of Cat's Meat Square had resulted in a loss to the local traders when the site was empty. While he appears to have followed the vestry line, there is no evidence he was either a house farmer or an active associate of the likes of George Gordon. Nathan Robinson, former chair of the Sanitary Committee and then a Progressive on the LCC also defended the vestry, saying during an LCC debate that it had been 'very badly treated'.[33] The vestry eventually accepted the two additional inspectors originally proposed, but the damage to St Pancras' reputation had been done.

Reynolds Newspaper published an article[34] during this furore which was extraordinary even by the vituperative standards of the time: 'St Pancras appears to be the foulest parish in all London. It is indeed a veritable slum....Shame on the disgraceful Vestry responsible for this outrage on civilisation! The whole of London must point the finger of scorn at such a disreputable public body, and ask if it is in league with the loathsome and criminal house-sweaters and rack-renters, most of whom ought to be in goal. When will the mean Cockney wake up to a sense of his rights and his responsibilities? St Pancras is the Filth-hole and Sewage-yard of London.'

George Bernard Shaw was quoted[35] as saying at a public meeting in June 1900 that the Local Government Board should make the vestries carry out the work so 'the vestrymen could go to their constituents with tears in their eyes and say they were compelled to spend the money'. At one of the final vestry meetings, held in March 1900, a question was asked[36] as to whether there was any probability that the vestry would be in a position to start building on Prospect Terrace or the other two sites that had been 'under consideration since 1891'. The Chairman of the Health Committee replied that there was 'no chance of commencing the buildings' by the demise of the vestry. In November 1900, St Pancras Vestry ceased to exist, having avoided laying a single brick of new housing. The fault cannot have been solely that of the vestry, but it did itself no favours by holding out so consistently against the tide of sanitary reform.

Notes, chapter 9

1 *The Standard*,
8 December 1885.

2 Minutes of the School
Board for London,
11 March 1886, p 603
(LMA).

3 Ibid, 28 October 1886,
p 1057 (LMA).

4 *The Standard*,
7 November 1884.

5 Minutes of the School
Board for London,
February 1886 (LMA).

6 Ibid, 1886-8.

7 Ibid, 27 February 1890.

8 *The Times*, 1885, 1887, 1888;
The Standard, 28 April 1887.
The 1885 sale was 'By order
of the Mortgagees', with
Daniel Alfred Harrison to be
Tenant for Life; he may have
already initiated disposal of
the Estate.

9 Sale of shares in Harrison
Estates Ltd, *The Times*,
January 1902.

10 Architect's drawings,
1887-8, LCC/AR/SCH/063
(LMA).

11 *The Standard*,
25 October 1990.

12 *Pall Mall Gazette*,
14 November 1891.

13 1891 England Census,
National Archives
(Ancestry.co.uk).

14 SPV Minutes,
2 November 1898 (CLSAC).

15 *Lloyd's Weekly Newspaper*,
6 November 1902.

16 *The Standard*,
7 January 1893.

17 *Reynold's Newspaper*,
14 July 1889.

18 *British Medical Journal*,
26 April 1890.

19 *Reynold's Newspaper*,
2 February 1890.

20 Report of the Enquiry
on behalf of the Secretary of
State by D Cubitt
Nichols, 1891 (CLSAC),
and *The Morning Post*,
1 November 1893.

21 SPV minutes,
16 November 189
(CLSAC).

22 *Daily News*,
March 1893.

23 *Morning Post*,
1 November 1893.

24 SPV minutes,
8 January 1896 (CLSAC).

25 SPV minutes,
30 January 1895 (CLSAC).

26 SPV minutes,
1 September 1897 (CLSAC).

27 Report from Dr J F Sykes,
SPV minutes, 24 November
1897 (CLSAC).

28 SPV minutes,
30 March 1898 (CLSAC).

29 Report by Dr William Hamer,
LCC, *The Sanitary Condition
and Administration of
the Parish of St Pancras*,
13 October 1898 (included
in the Report of the Special
Committee, SPV,
16 May 1899 (CLSAC)

30 *The Times*,
7 December 1898.

31 Report of the
Special Committee, SPV,
16 May 1899 (CLSAC).

32 *The Daily News*,
17 March 1899.

33 *The Morning Post*,
2 August 1899.

34 *Reynold's Newspaper*,
1 January 1899.

35 *The Daily News*,
29 June 1900.

36 SPV minutes,
14 March 1900 (CLSAC).

10 The end of Cat's Meat Square

(Notes for this chapter on p 75)

The new century opened with the inquest into the death of Rose Walters (p 33). The court had heard that Cat's Meat Square was 'about to come down', to which the coroner's officer, PC Bray, replied that it had been 'about to come down' for the last twenty years. He added 'there is not a worse or more overcrowded spot in St Pancras probably than the Wellington Place and Prospect Terrace area'.[1] The start of the borough council era would create fresh impetus later that year, but Cat's Meat Square was not yet about to come down and George Gordon was still collecting his rents.

Charles Booth in completing his great study *The life and labour of the people in London* in 1903 noted sweeping changes in the area west of Gray's Inn Road. He remarked[2] that the people generally were neither disreputable nor criminal, 'poor folk, but not bad; patient and long suffering'. Although there was less poverty, what remained was worse, with more overcrowding. For Cat's Meat Square, the 1899 edition of the Poverty Map of London retained the dark blue colouration edged with black of the 1889 version. Booth's researcher had toured the Prospect Terrace area and adjacent streets in July 1898 with PC Robert Turner. On turning into Derry Street they noted it was 'very rough. Costers. Irish predominate...all doors open, children dirty, ragged, four boys barefoot, one child with only a shirt.... Bricks thrown down on police from housetops'. 'No one lives in the basements though a good many make a free night's lodging out of it'.[3] Although Dr Sykes was apparently having some success in closing down basement dwellings, they were still being used for unofficial sleeping accommodation by people who would then be absent from the statistics.

In Prospect Terrace 'a great mess in the street' is recorded [25] 'the parish will not clean the road, hence its filthy state – a disgrace'.[3] Finally, 'the worst spot on this walk is without question Derry Street and Prospect Place'. The vestry also had to deal with the problem of the unpaved Prospect Terrace roadway (p 11) and eventually took out a magistrate's summons against the Rev Dacre Craven of St George the Martyr in 1896 for failing to keep the roadway clean.[4] This was not a new problem; in 1884, 5-year-old Margaret Ready had been rushed to the Royal Free Hospital having 'drank from the gutter'; she had been 'poisoned by carbolic acid which had been put down by parish workmen'.[5]

The two St Georges tried repeatedly to sell the roadway to the vestry, asking as much as £11,000. In 1893 they put it on the open market, claiming that it was 'most eligible for the erection of stabling, workshops etc'[6], the idea being to narrow the road to 10 ft. St Pancras Borough Council eventually bought the roadway in 1906 for £1,600 – a price still regarded by councillors as extortionate – and incorporated it into the new housing scheme.[7]

Booth's reference to greater overcrowding is supported by the 1901 census.[8]

The population had risen from 590 in 1891 to 695 and the density per house was now 18.3 persons. Had the School Board not taken some of the land, the numbers would certainly have topped 1000, or 1500 per acre, an appallingly high figure for such small houses. As people were unofficially sleeping in the basements[3] and undoubtedly on staircases, the actual night-time density must have been over 20, almost double the 1841 figure. The total number of households was now 178, the same as in 1841 even though a third of the houses had been demolished. Irish-born heads of households were now an insignificant 3.5%, but Booth's researcher three years earlier had claimed that the 'Irish predominate' in Derry Street – actually of course the Cockney Irish of at least the second or third generation. There were indeed many Irish surnames.

In February 1901 Dr Sykes again proposed that the Prospect Terrace and Derry

Street houses be placed on the tenements register to control overcrowding. The Health Committee of the new borough council inspected the properties, which they found to be in 'a most insanitary condition'. Rather than put them on the register, it was decided[9] that the sanitary inspectors should inspect the houses every three months and serve whatever notices were necessary – in effect continuing the ineffectual practice of previous decades. Cat's Meat Square was now at its most overcrowded, and the buildings were crumbling. The Borough of St Pancras had every reason to press on with the new housing schemes.

Work started on Goldington Buildings in late 1901. The intention was to complete the development before either Prospect Terrace or Brantome Place was pulled down, to mitigate the displacement from the demolitions; Brantome Place would then be rebuilt, followed finally by Prospect Terrace. Goldington Buildings were designed by Keith Young and were completed in 1903, providing accommodation for 332 people. First refusal for places was theoretically available for residents of Churchway and the other two sites, but this was never realistic. Even though space was provided for costermongers' barrows, it was inconceivable that these people would be able to commit to the rents, between 10s and 14s a week. From the 1911 census, it is clear the flats quickly filled with workers in steady jobs, much as had been the case with previous developments by the likes of Peabody. It is unlikely therefore that any real relief was felt in either Prospect Terrace or Brantome Place but St Pancras did at least have a new block of decent dwellings.

Early in the century the social reformer Mary Ward, who ran the Passmore Edwards Settlement in Tavistock Place, set up an evening play centre in Prospect Terrace School, having noticed that the local children could not be enticed out of their area. She donated money for toys and equipment. Writing 20 years later, one of her volunteers, Mrs Carwen, wrote that 'those who were kind enough to help us at the beginning will remember the wild yells which greeted us from a crowd of 50 children of all ages'. She recalled the 'old tenement houses long ago condemned (which) were inhabited by a population consisting mostly of hawkers of baked potatoes and chestnuts, stale fish and "trimmed vegetables". Numerous families occupied every house – a family in each room or at the outside two rooms. Broken windows, dilapidated stairs on which it was hardly safe to trust oneself, and broken doors which would neither open nor shut properly. In the basements stood tubs of water in which the potatoes and vegetables had been washed; rotting vegetables lay about in the gutters, and in these same gutters played some of the most lovable and fascinating children God ever made'.[10]

Mary Ward herself, in a long letter to *The Times* in 1906, wrote 'These children, many of them Irish, with their quick, responsive, affectionate natures, are admirable material; it will be the fault of the community if they are allowed to

[26] North Crescent Mews looking south west, by the entrance from Mabledon Place and just east of Brantome Place; its population was similar to that of Prospect Terrace, with a good many costermongers, labourers and charwomen.

go to ruin. Perhaps some objector will reply – "It will be the fault of the parents!" Well, let anyone who thinks that this settles the question go and study for himself the conditions of life in Derry Street'.[11] Figures such as the Duke of Bedford were keen to be associated with these efforts, and the Countess of Lovelace started a weekly class to teach the older boys how to mend their shoes. By 1904 the children were attending the Settlement itself, leading to a 'general improvement in manners and discipline'. The success of the Derry Street Play Centre led directly to the establishment, with the help of the LCC, of eight more such centres in other poor parts of London.

Mrs Ward also set up the Derry Street Factory Girls Club in 1905, 'intended for the lower type of factory girl'. In 1909, it was reported that attendance from the now-dispersed girls was still good, with an average of 35 meeting in the library at Tavistock Place for classes on clothes-making followed by dancing and games.[12]

With Goldington Buildings open, Brantome Place and North Crescent Mews [26] were cleared during 1905. It was claimed the following year[13] that many of the displaced people had 'crowded into the houses in Little Clarendon Street', in Somers Town. Work on the new block was delayed until 1906 by negotiations with the Skinners' Company, who owned some of the land. The building, to be named Flaxman Terrace Dwellings and housing 432 people, was designed by Joseph and Smithem, prolific architects of municipal housing in the late Victorian and Edwardian period. Much of their work survives and some of their buildings are listed. Solid and well built, Flaxman Terrace was designed in the Arts and Crafts style and was fully open only in 1908. Such was the mounting opprobrium about the state of the houses and the overcrowding in Prospect Terrace, however, that the decision to demolish Cat's Meat Square only after Flaxman Terrace opened was called into question.

St Pancras proceeded to buy up the remaining freehold and leasehold interests of the Prospect Terrace site, at an estimated cost in March 1901 of nearly £18,000, half being paid by the LCC. By June 1905 the borough was the landlord; George Gordon retired to Finchley and died later that year. The question was what rent should be charged to the hapless residents while the houses were still standing. Dr Sykes produced a table of rents which reduced the maximum sum payable from the 4s 6d a week charged by the house farmers for a single room to 3s, and forbade the occupation of basements. The maximum number permitted to sleep in the largest rooms was three, with one or two in the smaller rooms.[14] For the first time, the borough of St Pancras was applying the provisions of the tenements register to Prospect Terrace; but it was now in the unenviable position of being a slum landlord, a situation it would want to end as soon as possible.

In April 1906 the council resolved that the deteriorating conditions at Prospect Terrace [27] were such that the site should be cleared before Flaxman Terrace was ready.

The houses were now stated to be 'unfit for human habitation' – which of course had been the case for many years. It was agreed[15] that 'the number and rental of the rooms to let in Ward 8 be ascertained' for the use of the displaced occupants. A sixth of the tenants of the Prospect Terrace area were given notice to quit over each of three successive weeks. Magistrate's orders were taken out for those who did not comply. But finding alternative accommodation was inevitably difficult, especially for those with irregular earnings.[15]

On 16 May 1906, Alderman W H Matthews, who evidently felt he had a duty to his neighbours across Gray's Inn Road, brought a deputation of Prospect Terrace tenants to the council meeting. They presented a petition signed by 139 people 'protesting against the evictions with which they are threatened'. Philip Wilson, Liberal MP for St Pancras South since January of that year, spoke on behalf of the deputation. He said the tenants did not disagree with clearing the area but that 'there

were several hundred who had the greatest difficulty in obtaining other rooms, and even in the cases where they were prepared to pay the high rent asked elsewhere, when they told where they came from, they were refused rooms altogether.' He pressed for a delay in forcing the evictions. Asked if 'a few weeks' grace' would assist them, a member of the deputation replied 'That would be a great thing'. However, Councillor Beaton (who was also a Progressive LCC member) opposed any delay in enforcing the notices. He disingenuously pointed to the fact that the occupiers of Cat's Meat Square a few years previously had been offered flats in Goldington Buildings and had declined them. He said that 'this place was a disgrace to St Pancras and London and must be cleared'. Whilst the meeting was generally sympathetic to the tenants, the issue was conveniently referred to the Health Committee.[16]

Four weeks later the Health Committee reported to the full council meeting that further investigations had shown that the number of vacant rooms in the neighbourhood was 'several times greater than that required to accommodate the tenants', although it acknowledged that rents were about double that of Prospect Terrace, partly because of the council's reductions. Councillor Horne and Alderman Matthews appealed for more time but Councillor Beaton said the tenants 'wanted it all on their side' and referred to the fact that £250 in rent was owed to the borough. On a vote of 15:5, it was agreed to enforce the notices and 'That the remaining tenants of Prospect Terrace, Derry Street and Wellington Square, be required to remove before the end of July next'.[17]

Philip Wilson raised the evictions in the House of Commons via a written question[18] to the Local Government Board asking 'whether any arrangements have been made for re-housing these people at a reasonable rent'. The reply (from John Burns, by now a Liberal and who was not sympathetic to the residents of Cat's Meat Square, see p 60) simply referred to Goldington Buildings as alternative accommodation and said that 'it does not appear to me that the Board can do anything further in the matter'. The evictions proceeded, and at the council meeting on 25 July[19] it was reported that 'all the houses in Prospect Terrace are empty and by the end of next week all the houses on the south side of Derry Street will also be empty'. The Borough Engineer was instructed to demolish the houses 'with all possible expedition'. The last tenants left on Saturday 28 July and the house-breakers moved in on the following Monday.[20] By the end of the summer Cat's Meat Square had gone.

The whole matter had become an acute embarrassment to St Pancras, just when it was throwing off the old vestry reputation for penny-pinching and collusion with house farmers. It was therefore inevitable that the area was cleared quickly, but still an irony given that 15 years had passed since the re-housing scheme was first proposed. It was also apparent that an element of the 'undeserving poor' argument still persisted so that it was expedient to blame the tenants for their own predicament. Prospect Terrace was in a rapid spiral of decline, much like Poplar Place 20 years before, and electoral rolls provide some evidence that the more astute residents were already on the move by 1905, finding alternative rooms in the locality. That the petition had only 139 signatures (even allowing for illiteracy) and that Wilson referred to 'several hundred', suggests that the population in 1906 had appreciably dropped below the 695 recorded in 1901. However, Alderman Matthews claimed some years later[21] that 621 had been displaced. But where did they all go?

Comparison of the 1901 and 1911 censuses and examination of the electoral rolls for the period in between[22] provides a sample large enough to establish the dispersal pattern of those displaced from Cat's Meat Square. The number of insanitary areas in south St Pancras with 'cheap' accommodation had declined, leaving Somers Town as the most likely destination. But other changes were taking place, in particular the 'respectable' working class was increasingly fleeing to the suburbs. The widely held theory that those in the worst accommodation would migrate into the vacated better tenements, Georgian and early Victorian terraced houses, had some validity. The Health Committee had claimed, moreover, that the number of vacant rooms was 'several times greater' than the size of the displaced population. The natural turnover of rooms would mean there was always a fair number available, but the point missing from the council statement was that the number chasing each room was also large, and in many cases they were out of the poor tenants' price range.

The statement that the Brantome Place clearance had led to an influx into Somers Town, in particular Little Clarendon Street, is supported by evidence of the same process happening in the case of Prospect Terrace. A number of its former residents can be found there, both immediately after the demolition and on the 1911 census. The Ward 8 clearances therefore did have a direct, negative impact on Somers Town and added to the pressure for slum clearance there in the 1920s. Other families found their way to insanitary areas of Clerkenwell, especially the group of streets immediately east of Farringdon Road around present-day Margery Street. Again, these were the subject of clearances in the 1920s. There is also a detectable trend towards the Pentonville area of Islington and further north into Barnsbury.

Former Cat's Meat Square residents could be found all over south Pancras, from the Tottenham Court Road area to Judd Street, and further south around Theobalds Road. But the largest sample stayed very close and simply migrated to the surrounding streets – Cromer Street, Wakefield Street, Seaford Street, Harrison Street, and particularly Sidmouth Street. At least ten houses in Sidmouth Street took in Prospect Terrace tenants in the five years after 1906, especially of more established families rather than the more transient population. Cat's Meat Square may have been dead, but its soul was alive and well and living in Sidmouth Street.

Sidmouth Street was a respectable address in the early 19th century but by mid-century it was showing some signs of use as tenements, though it was not regarded as a slum. It always had a lower status than Regent Square, which was separated from it by gates (removed by Act of Parliament in 1890 along with three others on the Bedford Estate[23]). By the advent of the 20th century it was increasingly the preserve of working-class tenements, as was Harrison Street. Regent Square hung on to a middle-class air right up to WWII, and oral histories recorded in the King's Cross Voices project[24] refer to it as being 'posh'. By 1911 there were examples of overcrowding in Sidmouth Street.[25] No.27, for example, had 31 people living in it and No.7 had 29. The houses were larger and better built, and the norm had become renting a whole floor (two rooms and a landing), but there would still be only one WC in the house and no bathroom. As the houses had a dozen or so rooms, the density was about the same as in former Prospect Terrace. This 'better class' of slum would provide a significant proportion of London's housing stock right up to the 1960s.

Meanwhile, St Pancras had an empty site at Prospect Terrace and needed to make progress in filling it. The borough was already having second thoughts about the Keith Young plan, three storeys in height, which would now house 140 people (reduced from the original 200 and four storeys). The proposed flats were of the 'associated' type, with shared WCs and washhouses, increasingly seen as unsatisfactory. Clearly impressed by Joseph and Smithem's work, the council agreed in March 1907 to instruct the firm to design blocks to accommodate more families. In June the new design was approved.[26] It was to house 353 people in a mixture of 34 two-bedroom and 36 three-bedroom flats, lit by gas, with their own WCs but with a separate shared bathhouse. This was on the lower floors of the superintendent's block, at the entrance to Prospect Terrace (p 75). The two new tenement blocks were six storeys in height, constructed of red Leicester brick with artificial stone dressings, broadly in the Arts and Crafts style [28]. The cost of construction was £19,000, met with a loan from the Ecclesiastical Commissioners repayable over 60 years.[27]

Construction began in November 1908, more than two years after the site was cleared. On the afternoon of Tuesday 20 April the following year the great and the good of St Pancras assembled for the foundation stone ceremony. Several speakers referred to the length of time that had elapsed since the scheme was first conceived, and Alderman Matthews noted that he was one of only six active members of the old 120-strong vestry from that time. He said that the houses on the site had, in some cases, been in the ownership of the same families for 150 [sic] years and that the last legal exchanges had taken place three weeks earlier. No doubt the complex web of leases and under-leases that had built up over the years required much effort

[28] Prospect Terrace Dwellings, southern elevation. Photograph commissioned by the St Pancras Ironworks, who supplied the gates and railings. The two blocks were six storeys high and the roadway was now paved for the first time in its history.

[29] Prospect Terrace public baths and caretaker's lodge. Gray's Inn Road is just out of sight to the right. The backs of Sidmouth Street houses are just visible behind.

to unpick. Ever the shopkeeper, he also pointed out that the empty site had resulted in a 'great and serious loss' to the traders of the district. Councillor Blount made the point that 'many who had been turned out of the buildings had gone to swell the already overcrowded in other parts'.[28]

The buildings were finished within six months and on 26 October 1909, braving an 'incessant downpour of rain', councillors and MPs again assembled for the opening ceremony. The speeches were 'delivered in almost semi-darkness' due to the inclement weather.[29] Councillor Hewitt, Chairman of the Health Committee, referred to this being the third new housing development in St Pancras and that 'they had done something the last three years which should have been done previously'. Captain H M Jessel noted that 'although they would not be able to take in the submerged tenth which were cleared out of them, of course a better class of working men and women would take them, and the others would be able to take their places'. Alderman Matthews declared that 'the buildings were intended to last 200 years and they would be paid for in sixty'. Mr Joseph, the architect, then handed the key to the mayor 'who unlocked the main door and declared the buildings open' [28, 29].

The rents for the new flats ranged from 7s for two rooms on the top floor to

12s for three rooms with the best outlook – and, as expected, by 1910 they were occupied by policemen, postmen and others with secure jobs and reasonable wages. It was decided[30] that the baths should be open to the public as well as to tenants, at a cost of 2d, or 4d including towels and soap. Having separate baths (and charging the tenants to use them) was by 1909 rather out of date, and after WWI integral baths increasingly became the norm in new housing. St Pancras was now the owner of three new sets of dwellings and in less than a decade had gone from one of the worst local authorities in London in the matter of housing to one of the better. It was regrettable, though, that the very poor could not avail themselves of the new facilities and faced many years of substandard housing.

Notes, chapter 10

1 *Daily News*,
   3 January 1900.

2 Booth, Charles.
   *Life and Labour of the
   People in London*,
   Third Series,
   Vol 2, p 170, 1902.

3 Charles Booth Online
   Archive, B354,
   pp 55-56 (London
   School of Economics).

4 SPV minutes,
   26 February 1896
   (CLSAC).

5 *Illustrated Police News*,
   25 October 1884.

6 *The Standard*,
   4 May 1893.

7 St Pancras Borough
   Council (SPBC)
   minutes,
   11 July 1906
   (CLSAC).

8 1901 England Census,
   National Archives
   (Ancestry.co.uk).

9 SPBC minutes,
   5 February 1901.

10 Carwen, C.
   'The Derry Street Play
   Centre', in *In Memoriam:
   Mrs Humphry Ward
   and the Passmore
   Edwards Settlement*,
   1921 (LMA).

11 *The Times*,
   5 February 1906.

12 Annual report No.11,
   Passmore Edwards
   Settlement
   (LMA 4524/B/02/001).

13 Philip Wilson MP,
   SPBC minutes,
   16 May 1906 (CLSAC).

14 Report to SPBC
   by Dr J F Sykes,
   4 January 1905 (CLSAC).

15 SPBC minutes,
   25 April 1906 (CLSAC).

16 SPBC minutes,
   16 May 1906
   and *St Pancras Gazette*,
   May 1906.

17 SPBC minutes,
   13 June 1906
   and *St Pancras Gazette*, June
   1906.

18 Hansard, 14 June 1906,
   Vol 158, pp 1114-5.

19 SPBC minutes,
   25 July 1906 (CLSAC).

20 *Devon and Exeter Gazette*,
   31 July 1906.

21 *St Pancras Gazette*,
   22 April 1909.

22 1901 England Census, 1911
   England Census, National
   Archives and London
   Electoral Rolls
   (LMA and Ancestry.co.uk).

23 The London Streets
   (Removal of Gates) Act 1890.

24 King's Cross Voices Project:
   Queenie Chapman,
   2005 (CLSAC).

25 1911 England Census,
   National Archives
   (Ancestry.co.uk).

26 SPBC minutes,
   5 June 1907 (CLSAC).

27 *St Pancras Gazette*,
   14 May 1909.

28 *St Pancras Gazette*,
   23 April 1909.

29 *St Pancras Gazette*,
   29 October 1909.

30 SPBC minutes,
   15 December 1909.

Epilogue: Cat's Meat Square in the 20th century
(Notes to the Epilogue on p 78)

The years immediately after 1910 were unremarkable in the Prospect Terrace Dwellings. In Sidmouth Street, former residents of Cat's Meat Square brought up their families, sent their children to Prospect Terrace School and made use of the bathing facilities around the corner. The derogatory name faded out locally, although the Rev Ensor Walters was still using "Cat's Meat Square" as an example of iniquity as he toured the country in 1918.[1] After WWI, Sidmouth Street, itself now regarded as overcrowded, was earmarked for clearance, but Somers Town took priority and nothing happened.

World War II was to bring fundamental change, and Alderman Matthews' prediction that the new Prospect Terrace flats would last 200 years would not come to fruition. Because St Pancras Ward 8 was close to major railway termini, it was subject to intense bombing. In October 1940 the Luftwaffe made increasing use of parachute mines, a particularly deadly weapon. On the night of 15/16 October, eight parachute mines hit south St Pancras and four of them exploded. The first hit Cromer Street at 3.15 am, flattening a large number of shops and houses and killing eight people. At 3.50 am a second parachute mine scored a direct hit on Prospect Terrace.[2] The main block, facing Prospect Terrace itself, was virtually demolished and the second block along Wellington Place was severely damaged, as was the school. Thirty-two people died, making it one of the worst Blitz incidents in St Pancras. One of the deaths in Prospect Terrace was that of Michael Ryan, normally resident at No.10 Sidmouth Street, where ironically there were no fatalities despite much blast damage.[3]

[30] Nos.27-35 Sidmouth Street in 1943, with the Prince Regent pub to the right. The top floors of the terrace have been blown off. Visible just behind is one of the corner turrets of Prospect Terrace School and the Wellington Place block of the flats.

As the flats were known to be well built with steel and concrete floors, many inhabitants had a false sense of security and stayed at home or took shelter in the lower levels, together with people from surrounding streets, including Michael Ryan. Such was the intensity of the blast that the flats were reduced to rubble and twisted metal; bodies were still being recovered on 31 October.[4] Sidmouth Street was largely destroyed by the blast: this is vividly illustrated by an LCC photograph three years later [30] showing several houses and the Prince Regent pub on the south side. The top floors have been scythed off and only the façade of the lower storeys survived. A few years later, all the damaged buildings had been cleared away, including the flats, baths, school and all but eleven houses on Sidmouth Street.

In 1946, new education plans for the post-war period were drawn up and a 1500-place county secondary school was planned on an expanded Prospect Terrace site, 3.5 acres in extent, to be achieved by the demolition of Heathcote Street, Mecklenburgh Street and most of Mecklenburgh Square, with 2.5 acres of Coram's Fields annexed for school use. The borough's ownership of the Prospect Terrace flats site was swapped with that of the bomb-damaged Cromer Street School. Mercifully, the large school proposal was abandoned and Mecklenburgh Square was saved from destruction.[5]

The LCC opted instead for a smaller, further education building on a Prospect Terrace site enlarged by taking in the south side of Sidmouth Street. Intended for Kingsway College, the new building was designed by Ron Herron and Peter Nicholls of the LCC architects' department and was constructed in 1957-8. It cleverly used some basement spaces of the former flats and houses for sunken gardens, and the grounds extended south across most of Prospect Terrace itself down to Heathcote Street, turning the triangular site into a rectangle. The college buildings served for a while as a secondary school addressing the needs of the 11-year-olds who were the outcome of the post-war baby boom. Starcross School used the site until 1965, when it was merged with the scandal-hit Risinghill School in Islington and moved to the latter's site, taking the Starcross name with it.[6] That school, now known as Elizabeth Garrett Anderson Girls' School, is famous for the patronage of Michelle Obama.

A further building in the brutalist style was added in 1974, along the Gray's Inn Road frontage. This finally saw the end of the name 'Prospect Terrace', as the new building was erected across the 25% of the original street still extant. All traces of the historic access road to the burial grounds and Harrison's unusual development were eliminated.

From 2007 Westminster Kingsway College redeveloped the site again, with two blocks of flats to the south of Sidmouth Street overlooking St George's Gardens due to be erected in 2012. Thus housing has, ironically, returned to Cat's Meat Square 200 years after the first terraces were erected.

Notes, Epilogue

1 *Western Daily Press*, 24 June 1918.

2 Newberry, Charles Allen. *Wartime St Pancras*, p 23 (Camden History Society 2006).

3 Commonwealth War Graves Commission (CWGC.org).

4 Mee family probate records, National Probate Calendar (Ancestry.co.uk).

5 LCC Education Committee minutes, 18 December 1946 (LMA).

6 *Education*, Vol 125, p 284, 1965.

Index